GUIDE TO
the
Fairy Ring

About the Creators

Anna Franklin (England) has been collecting fairy lore for many years. She has been a practicing Pagan for thirty years and a High Priestess for sixteen. She now works as a teacher, photographer, artist, and writer. Anna appears in *The Fairy Ring* as the Lake Maiden and as the Green Lady.

Paul Mason (England) is a professional artist and photographer. He appears in *The Fairy Ring* as King Finvarra. Anna and Paul are also the creators of *The Sacred Circle Tarot*.

To Write to the Author

If you wish to contact the author or would like more information about this book, please write to the author in care of Llewellyn Worldwide and we will forward your request. Both the author and publisher appreciate hearing from you and learning of your enjoyment of this book and how it has helped you. Llewellyn Worldwide cannot guarantee that every letter written to the author can be answered, but all will be forwarded. Please write to:

Anna Franklin
℅ Llewellyn Worldwide
P.O. Box 64383, Dept. 0-7387-0274-9
St. Paul, MN 55164-0383, U.S.A.
Please enclose a self-addressed stamped envelope for reply,
or $1.00 to cover costs. If outside U.S.A., enclose
international postal reply coupon.

Many of Llewellyn's authors have websites with additional information and resources. For more information, please visit our website at http://www.llewellyn.com.

GUIDE TO
the Fairy Ring

WRITTEN BY
ANNA FRANKLIN

ILLUSTRATED BY
PAUL MASON

2002
Llewellyn Publications
St. Paul, Minnesota 55164-0383, U.S.A.

First Edition
Second Printing, 2002

Book design by Donna Burch
Cover art © 2002 by Paul Mason
Cover design by Kevin R. Brown
Editing by Andrea Neff
Interior art © 2002 by Paul Mason and Kevin R. Brown (p. 22)

Additional photography by Anna Franklin

ISBN 0-7387-0274-9
Library of Congress Cataloging-in-Publication Data (Pending)

Llewellyn Publications
A Division of Llewellyn Worldwide, Ltd.
P.O. Box 64383, Dept. 0-7387-0274-9
St. Paul, MN 55164-0383, U.S.A.
www.llewellyn.com

 Printed in the United States of America on recycled paper

For Harry Mason and Sue Phillips

Acknowledgments

Many thanks to Donna, Barbara, Lynne, and Andrea
for their hard work on this project,
and a special thanks to Kevin
for his excellent cover design.

Other Works by Anna Franklin

Midsummer
(Llewellyn, 2002)

Real Wicca for Teenagers
(Capall Bann, 2002)

The Illustrated Encyclopaedia of Fairies
with Paul Mason & Helen Field, illustrators
(Chrysalis, 2002)

Lammas
with Paul Mason, coauthor
(Llewellyn, 2001)

Magical Incenses and Oils
(Capall Bann, 2000)

The Wellspring
(Capall Bann, 2000)

Fairy Lore
with Paul Mason, illustrator
(Capall Bann, 2000)

Personal Power
(Capall Bann, 1998)

The Sacred Circle Tarot: A Celtic Pagan Journey
with Paul Mason, illustrator
(Llewellyn, 1998)

Pagan Feasts
(Capall Bann, 1997)

Familiars: The Animal Powers of Britain
(Capall Bann, 1997)

Herb Craft
(Capall Bann, 1995)

Contents

The Autumn Court

The Winter Court

The Fairy Festival Cards

Sample Spreads

INTRODUCTION

In the cards of *The Fairy Ring*, you will find beautiful fairies and ugly fairies, good fairies and wicked fairies, helpful creatures and mischievous beings who will try to trick you and lead you astray. We have gathered them all together to form this divination deck where each fairy may work its own particular magic for you.

Today, people are as interested in fairies as they ever were, though most now think of them as amusing myths. However, only a few hundred years ago, belief in fairies was absolute in every strata of society. Gradually this notion dwindled among town dwellers and so-called "sophisticated" people, but country folk well into the twentieth century worried about offending the fairies. Building on a fairy path, digging into a fairy mound, forgetting to leave out cream, or omitting to pour milk on a fairy stone, all of these things and more could incur the wrath of the Little People. The crops might be ruined, the cows might sicken and the milk dry in the udder, the family might be cursed with bad luck, the baby stolen and replaced by a withered changeling, or the breadwinner paralyzed by an elf stroke.

If the fairies are treated with respect and given their due, they will help those who honor them, and may bestow great gifts on their favorites. They can teach a bard how to play music that will move an audience to tears or have them dancing with joy. They can bestow the power of healing on a mortal. The famous witch Biddy Early (d. 1873) maintained that she derived her powers from the fairies. She used a blue bottle, given to her by them, for healing. At her death it was thrown into a lake.

During the persecutions, many witches insisted that their powers were derived from fairies, not devils, as their prosecutors insisted. In the north of England, a man was accused of witchcraft and trafficking with the devil to gain a medicinal white powder. The man contended that he had received the medicine from the fairies. He would go up to the fairy mound, knock three times, and the hill would open. He would then go inside and confer with the fairies, after which they would give him a white powder with which he was able to cure those who requested his aid. He offered to take the judge and jury to the fairy hill to see for themselves. The judge was unimpressed, but the jury refused to convict him.[1]

In Ireland, the young girls that fairies carried off for brides would be sent back to the human world when they grew old and ugly, but with the knowledge of herbs, philters, and secret spells to give them power over men.[2] In 1613, Isobel Halfdane of Perth in Scotland was carried from her bed into the fairy hills where she spent three days learning the secrets of witchcraft.

Fairies and witches were on good terms with each other, and witches were frequent visitors to the fairy hills; being accused of such visits was enough to secure a conviction as a witch. Witches were also known to grow many of the fairy plants (such as foxgloves, elder, primrose, thyme, and bluebells) in their gardens or to gather them from the wild to attract their fairy friends. At one time, even the presence of such plants in a garden was enough to warrant an accusation of witchcraft. Modern witches working in the traditional way still derive the greater part of their knowledge from the wildfolk spirits of the land.

Fairies hate idleness and are very hardworking. They will help favored humans around the house and farm, spinning, weaving, baking, churning, and building, or working as gold or silversmiths. This work is all done at night as the people sleep, as long as the house is left tidy and the hearth is swept, as fairies cannot tolerate dirt and mess. If the customary dish of cream is not left as the small reward the fairies require, then the helpful home sprite will be mortally offended and smash the crockery, wreck the spinning, and hide valuable objects. Fairies like luxury and have contempt for those who penny pinch, especially those who drain the last drop of milk from the churn or strip all the fruit from the trees, leaving none for the fairies. They punish kitchen maids who do not sweep the hearth clean and put out clean water for bathing fairy babies with pinches, cramps, and lameness, while conscientious maids are rewarded with money in their shoes and good luck.

In the past it was considered unlucky to name the fairies, or even to use the word *fairy*, perhaps because to do so may have summoned them, or because using a name without its owner's permission was a threat or challenge. It was wise to call them "the Good People," "the Little People," "the Gentry," "the Mother's Blessing," "Good Neighbors," "Wee Folk," or "the Hidden People."

The English word *fairy*, or *faerie*, is derived by way of the French *fée*, from the Latin *fatare*, meaning "to enchant." Variations on the spelling include fayerye, fairye, fayre, and faery. In England, Geoffrey Chaucer made the words *fairy* and *elf* interchangeable, though the word *elf* is from the Scandinavian *alfar,* a term that seems to mean "bright" or "shining."

Though this deck features fairies from Britain and Ireland, there are legends of fairies all over the world, from the tiny South African Abatwa, to the Japanese Chin-Chin Kobakama, the Arabian Djinn, the Russian Děduška Domovoi, the ancient Greek nymphs, and the Albanian Zera. I have been collecting legends of fairies for many years and have recorded over three thousand individuals, and realize that I have only uncovered the tip of the iceberg. Around the world, fairies are mysterious creatures who live apart from the race of humankind, but who are sometimes seen in wild and lonely places.

The Victorian view of fairies was that they were all delicate, miniature, butterfly-winged creatures, but in older legends they are of human or even giant size. In medieval lore, fairies came to be divided into the aristocracy, who appeared in groups, and the common fairies, who appeared individually. The common fairies were elusive, and often the only sign of their existence was in their passing, with the bending of the flowers or the rustling of the leaves in the branches, or the patterns of Jack Frost in the windowpane. They were the guardians of individual streams, trees, forests, pools, and streams, or sometimes of private houses and particular families. The aristocrats were called Heroic or Trooping Fairies in England, and belonged to the Seelie Courts of Scotland or the Daoine Sidhe (pronounced "Theena Shee") of Ireland. The Daoine Sidhe were believed to be the diminished remnants of the Tuatha dé Danaan ("People of the Goddess Dana"), driven underground by the Celtic invaders.

Fairies are often said to live beneath the ancient burial mounds, the Hollow Hills of lore, where they feast and dance. Sometimes at night these hills sparkle with light, and if you press an ear to the hill you will hear their revels. If you sleep on the mound, fairy music will enter your soul and you will never be the same again. Earthworks are also associated with fairies; it is said that when the ancient race moved out, the fairies moved in. No tree on them should be cut down, nor should anything be built on them. If a man should be rash enough to attempt either sacrilege, the fairies will blast his eyes or give him a crooked mouth.

The Fairy Ring is a divination deck that calls upon the powers of the fay to guide you and to give you a glimpse of what destiny has in store for you. All fairies can see into the future and are capable of bestowing the gift of prophecy on those they love, like the Fairy Boy of Leith, who had amazing powers of second sight, and who visited his fairy friends every Thursday at Calton Hill, near Edinburgh. The entrance to the hill was only visible to those with fairy gifts, and once inside, the boy joined in the revels, playing a drum for the fairies to dance to. Sometimes they all flew off to France or Holland for the evening. Once some men tried to keep the boy in conversation one Thursday evening, but despite all their efforts, the boy slipped away to keep his appointment with the People of the Hills.[3]

The fairy hills are calling, and the gateway to the Otherworld stands open. Its denizens are ready to take you by the hand and lead you into the Fairy Ring . . .

---

1. Durant Hotham, *Life of Jacob Behmen* (1654).

2. Lady Wilde, *Ancient Legends, Mystic Charms and Superstitions of Ireland* (London: Ward & Downey, 1887).

3. Captain George Burton, *Pandaemonium* (1684).

Using Your Cards

The Cards

The cards in the *Fairy Ring* deck are divided into four suits: Spring, Summer, Autumn, and Winter. Most fairies are seasonal creatures, and individual fairies are featured during the period when they are most likely to appear. The thirteen cards in each suit are numbered one to nine, with four court cards: Lady, Knave, Queen, and King. Each card features a different fairy, with fifty-two fairies in all.

In addition, there are eight festival cards marking the chief fairy feasts of Imbolc, Ostara, Beltane, Midsummer, Lughnasa, Herfest, Samhain, and Yule.

Reading the Cards

The cards should be shuffled by the person for whom the reading is to be made—this might be yourself, a friend, or a client, if you are a professional clairvoyant. I shall call this person "the questioner" for the sake of simplicity. The questioner should take care to reverse some of the cards, so that when they are laid out, they will be "upside down" (i.e., the top of the picture will be at the bottom). Like Tarot cards, the *Fairy Ring* cards have both upright and reversed meanings. While some Tarot readers prefer not to use reversed meanings, the *Fairy Ring* deck is specifically designed to employ both upright and reversed meanings, and only by using both will an accurate result be achieved.

The reader should take the shuffled cards from the questioner and lay them out, facedown, in the chosen spread. You will find a selection of spreads in the pages that follow. Some layouts will give you a quick answer to a single question; others will give you a more detailed life reading. Some spreads are better for practical matters, and others for emotional or spiritual concerns. I suggest that you read through the spreads and choose the one that appeals to you. The cards will also work well with your favorite Tarot spread.

When you are ready, begin at card one and turn it faceup. Note whether it is upright or reversed. When you are reading for yourself, you might like to look at the descriptions found under the heading "The Fairy," as this will give you insight into the characteristics and influences of each fairy. However, when you are reading for another person, it is not necessary to read this material to the person each time, unless you feel it would be particularly helpful; but you can just read the upright (divinatory) or reversed meanings as appropriate. Interpret each card before turning over the next. It is useful to summarize, in your own words, everything you have discovered at the end of the reading. As you become experienced and learn more about the fairy energies involved, you will find that additional interpretations occur to you. Don't be afraid to mention these; as with the Tarot, the given interpretations are only a starting point.

When you consider the meanings of the cards, bear in mind that any court card—a Knave, Lady, Queen, or King—may indicate real people in the life of the questioner. In addition, the appearance of one of the eight festival cards should be given extra weight in the interpretation of a spread. They indicate powerful trends that cannot be fought, but must be accepted and worked with. Occasionally—and this will have to be carefully considered—they might indicate a time period when an event might occur.

13

12   11

10   9   8   7

6   5   4   3   2   1

The Fairy Mound

The Fairy Mound spread will help you determine the important issues and events of your past, what influences and concerns have a bearing on the present, and how best to move into the future.

Shuffle the cards, taking care to invert some of them to make use of the reversed meanings. Lay out the cards according to the diagram, starting with card one and finishing with card thirteen. Begin your reading at card one:

1. This card best represents the questioner at the present time. Even if the card seems a little surprising, it will point to those aspects of the questioner that are currently most significant.

2. This card reveals the influences closest to the questioner at the present moment.

3. This card reveals what the questioner most desires.

4. This card reveals the questioner's mental processes as they relate to current events.

5. This card reflects the questioner's emotions.

6. Card six indicates past influences and trends that are still affecting present circumstances.

7. This card relates to spiritual questions and concerns.

8. Card eight concerns practical matters, money, and material issues.

9. This card indicates karmic events that cannot be avoided.

10. Card ten reveals important future influences, whether helpful or not.

11. This card indicates immediate concerns.

12. Card twelve advises the questioner on the best path to success.

13. Card thirteen indicates the outcome.

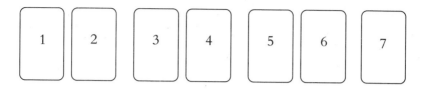

The Fairy Oracle

The Fairy Oracle spread may be used to find the answer to a single question.

Shuffle the cards, taking care to invert some of them to make use of the reversed meanings. Lay out the cards according to the diagram, starting with card one and finishing with card seven. Begin your reading at card one:

1. This card represents the questioner in his or her present circumstances. The card may be surprising, but some aspect of the card will reveal the truth of the situation.

2. This card discloses the nature of the questioner's most pressing query.

3. Card three makes known what influences may help the questioner.

4. Card four reveals what influences may hinder the questioner's desires.

5. This card indicates which course of action is the best to follow.

6. Card six reveals the root of the problem, which may lie in the distant past.

7. Card seven divulges the outcome of the situation in the near future.

In general, a greater number of upright cards indicates a *yes* answer, while a greater number of reversed cards indicates a *no*.

The Fairy Gifts

The Fairy Gift spread is used to ascertain what skills the questioner may call upon to fulfill his or her destiny, or what trends and obstacles are preventing him or her from doing so.

Shuffle the cards, taking care to invert some of them to make use of the reversed meanings. Lay out the cards according to the diagram, starting with card one and finishing with card five. Begin your reading at card one:

1. The questioner, or significant aspects of the questioner, at the present moment.

2. The questioner's innate talents that will aid him or her in gaining fulfillment.

3. Potentials as yet unrealized or untapped.

4. What will guide the questioner's choices.

5. Events in which fate or destiny takes a hand, for good or bad; perhaps problems that need to be overcome.

1

10 11

7 8 9

2 3 4 5

6

The Fairy Market

The Fairy Market spread is a versatile layout that may be used for general readings, or to determine answers to specific questions.

Shuffle the cards, taking care to invert some of them to make use of the reversed meanings. Lay out the cards according to the diagram, starting with card one and finishing with card eleven. Begin your reading at card one:

1. This card represents the questioner, or significant aspects of the questioner.

2. This card concerns the question.

3. Card three represents obstacles in the way of the questioner.

4. This card relates to the questioner's past.

5. Card five shows present trends surrounding the questioner.

6. Card six demonstrates what the questioner can expect in the near future.

7. This card predicts events or trends in the distant future.

8. This card indicates the mental aspects of the question.

9. This card advises the questioner as to what will help.

10. Card ten reveals what the questioner hopes or fears.

11. Card eleven reveals the final outcome.

12

11

1

10

2

9

3

8

4

7

5

6

The Year Spread

The Year Spread may be utilized to gain insight into what the current year holds for the questioner. It is best to perform this spread at the beginning of the year. If the spread is used midyear, some of the cards will relate to the past (those months of the year already past), one to the present (the current month), and some to the future.

Remove the eight festival cards from the pack: these are not used in this layout. Shuffle the cards, taking care to invert some of them to make use of the reversed meanings. Lay out the cards according to the diagram, starting with card one and finishing with card twelve.

Begin your reading at card one, which represents January; proceed to card two, which represents February; and carry on through the year to card twelve, which represents December. An interpretation of the general trends of each month is made from the twelve cards.

	Past	**Present**	**Future**
Mind	1	2	3
Body	4	5	6
Spirit	7	8	9
Emotions	10	11	12

The Life Reading

The Life Reading may be used when an in-depth analysis of the questioner's life and circumstances is required.

Shuffle the cards, taking care to invert some of them to make use of the reversed meanings. Lay out the cards according to the diagram, starting with card one and finishing with card twelve.

To give you a picture of the questioner's past, begin your reading at card one (past mental attitudes), next read card four (past health), then card seven (past spiritual concerns), and then card ten (past emotional concerns). Next read the cards in the "Present" column: cards two, five, eight, and eleven. Finally, read the cards in the "Future" column: cards three, six, nine, and twelve.

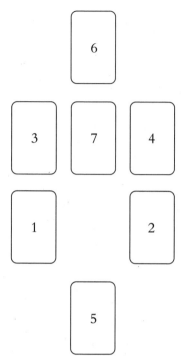

The Wildfolk Guides

According to the old teachings, witches learn all their secrets from the fairy wildfolk. The Wildfolk Guides spread helps you access those fairy energies that will help you throughout your life.

Remove the eight festival cards, as they are not used for this spread. Lay out the cards according to the diagram, beginning with card one and finishing with card seven. Begin reading at card one and finish with card seven. If you draw cards with negative implications, this is telling you that you are blocking some essential part of yourself or your connection to these energies. Any reading of this spread should be interpreted in this light.

1. The fairy guide at your left heel holds the key to accessing your most powerful wellspring of vitality, sensual pleasure, and raw instinct.

2. The fairy at your right heel is your guide to emotional well-being and boundless joy.

3. The guide at your left hand teaches you about personal balance and the use of the intellect.

4. The fairy companion at your right hand shows you the way to inner harmony and personal growth.

5. The guide behind you helps you access greater creativity and self-expression.

6. The guide before you opens the psychic senses, clairvoyance, imagination, and vision.

7. The guide at your heart holds the key to spiritual awareness and illuminates your path to eternal truth.

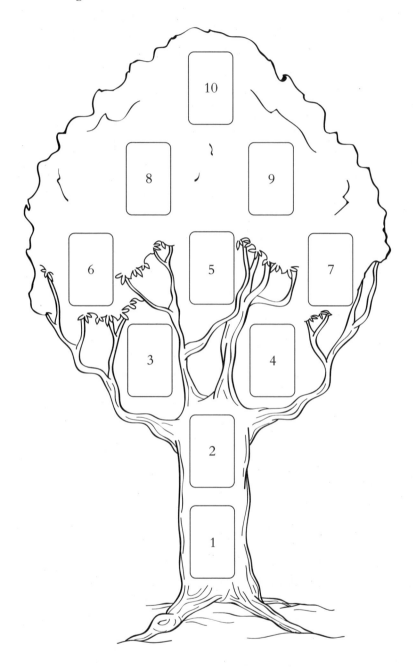

The Fairy Oak

The Fairy Oak Spread can be used when you wish to discover the root of an issue or problem, and determine how events and circumstances have progressed from this cause.

1. Card one relates to the physical world and material matters.

2. Card two indicates the root of the questioner's personality and approach, and his or her subconscious influences.

3. This card indicates the intellectual basis of the question and offers insights into the situation.

4. Card four deals with emotional matters, relationships, and love.

5. Card five deals with matters the questioner needs to bring into balance.

6. This card suggests what lessons need to be learned in order to grow and move forward.

7. This card indicates the best way the questioner can direct his or her energies.

8. Card eight reveals what the questioner intuitively knows.

9. Card nine points out any action the questioner needs to take.

10. Card ten reveals the heart of the matter.

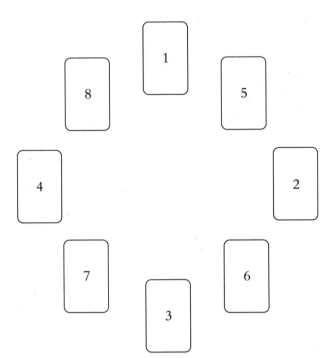

The Fairy Ring

The Fairy Ring Spread will give you an overview of your life trends, and insight on how best to move forward.

1. Card one reveals your current life phase.

2. Card two shows what is behind you.

3. Card three shows what is before you.

4. Card four indicates weaknesses to be overcome.

5. Card five shows strengths that need to be developed.

6. Card six indicates obstacles that lie in your way.

7. Card seven shows what will help you.

8. Card eight reveals the final outcome of this phase.

1

10   11

7   8   9

2   3   4   5

6

A Sample Reading

This sample reading uses the Fairy Market spread. The questioner was a middle-aged woman with teenage children.

1. The first card revealed was the Green Lady, who represented the questioner. This indicated a loving, resourceful woman who was loyal to her family, clever and enthusiastic, quick to anger, but also quick to love.

2. The second card revealed the principal reason the questioner sought a reading. The card was the Boggart, indicating trouble at the questioner's home involving family arguments, quarrels, and disruptions, probably involving a troublesome child or teenager.

3. Card three indicated obstacles in the way of the questioner. This card suggested that she was perhaps having difficulty with the lessons of Jenny Greenteeth—the necessity of letting go of one thing in order to gain another, flexibility, and the need to adapt to change.

4. Card four concerned the questioner's past. Béfind indicated that the questioner had many talents she hadn't used, leading to feelings of incompleteness and dissatisfaction.

5. Card five denoted the questioner's present circumstances. Queen Mab indicated dreams, wishes, and unfulfilled longings, but also new ideas and impulses.

6. Card six concerned the near future and was revealed as the Ace of the Winter Court, the Knocker. This suggested financial or material gain, and establishing a firm foundation in some practical matter.

7. Card seven related to the distant future. The Elder Queen indicated warmth, friendship, and the success of a venture.

8. Card eight revealed the mental aspects of the problem. When the Queen of the Autumn Court appears reversed in a spread, she indicates overwhelming emotions, mood swings, and emotional instability.

9. This card gives advice on what will help. When the kindly Tiddy Mun appears, he heralds new opportunities or the development of a venture that may bring material rewards. This card also indicated a real person in the life of the questioner, a charming young man with a mercurial temperament who is romantic, idealistic, chivalrous, freedom loving, and gentle.

10. Hopes and fears: The appearance of the Will o' the Wisp betokened illusion, falseness, delusion, fallacy, deception, trickery, self-delusion, wishful thinking, broken promises, and unreliability.

11. Outcome: Wayland Smith appeared in the cards to indicate a period of hard work, forging new things from the old, creation, craftsmanship, transmutation, opportunities and success at hand, knowledge, skill, and mastery.

The questioner was a middle-aged woman with a nearly grown-up family. She wanted to return to work as a designer, and had been offered a job by the young man she recognized in the Tiddy Mun card. However, she worried about whether this was the right course of action, as her teenage son was experiencing problems that manifested as disruptive behavior. She was afraid that her return to employment might exacerbate the situation, and that, as she put it herself, "he might go off the rails completely."

The Will o' the Wisp card suggested that the questioner's fears were greatly exaggerated, that her son was experiencing no more than normal teenage angst. She admitted that she had mixed feelings. On the one hand, she wished to express all those talents she had put on hold while she raised her family—as revealed by the

Béfind card—and on the other hand, she regretted that she was no longer needed on a twenty-four-hour-a-day basis by her family. The card of Jenny Greenteeth reminded her that there is a necessary process of letting go as children discover their own individuality and ready themselves to leave the nest. The questioner recognized that at least some of the family problems were caused by her trying to keep too tight a hold on her son.

The final card of Wayland Smith revealed that the woman would gain great pleasure, satisfaction, and success from her new career. While one phase of her life was drawing to an end, another exciting opportunity was hers for the taking.

Using the Cards for Meditation

Each of the sixty *Fairy Ring* cards can be used for meditation. The images act as a pictorial key to connect with the particular fairy energies involved, and the deck has been designed with this in mind.

Connecting with Fairy Energies

Take the card you have decided to work with and study the picture. Examine the elements that make up the image. Read about the fairy on the card. Hold the card in front of you and look at it again. When you feel you have the picture and the basic symbolism fixed in your mind, put the card down in front of you, close your eyes, and relax. You are going to enter into the card and interact with the fairy within.

For example, suppose you have chosen the Brownie. Close your eyes and relax. Imagine that you are in the warm kitchen of a cozy cottage, seated by the fire, toasting your toes. It is evening and getting dark outside. There is a wind rustling through the trees and whistling in the eaves, and you are glad to be inside. The kettle is on the stove, singing away, ready to make the tea. The fire

31

crackles and the comforting scent of wood smoke and baking bread fills the room.

You are starting to doze when you become aware of movement behind you, and the swishing of a broom. Keeping quite still, you open your eyes halfway, and before you, busy at her work, is a homely female brownie in a drab dress and pinafore.

This is the house fairy of the cottage; every good home should have one to protect it and see to its needs. You keep quiet as you do not want to frighten away the creature. You know that brownies do not like to be thanked, but only given a bowl of cream each night, and to have all the family news whispered up the chimney. You may silently watch the brownie for as long as you wish, and are aware that some subtle level of communication exists between you.

When you are ready to leave, feel yourself back in your own room with the card in front of you, and bring yourself back to waking consciousness. When you are ready, open your eyes.

It is a good idea to write down your experience as soon as possible. Keep a record of your meditations and you will be able to perceive any patterns and lessons that are emerging and understand where your path is taking you.

The next time you repeat the exercise, visualize your own home. Not everyone has an open fire today, but the center of the home is often the kitchen, where people gather to eat and talk. Imagine yourself sitting quietly in whatever place is the center of your home, until you catch a glimpse of your own home sprite, which may be quite different in appearance to the one illustrated in the *Fairy Ring* card.

To attract and honor a brownie, make an altar in a small wall niche or on the mantle shelf over the fireplace, since this is the traditional shrine of the house spirit. Place on it an image that represents the spirit, or something that you associate with the sanctity and work of the home. Place regular offerings of milk, wine, and flowers on the altar, especially at family gatherings and occasions. Tell the fairy all the family news. Never make demands, and place offerings on the altar instead of saying "thank you," which brownies don't like—where fairies are concerned, the mysteries should not be acknowledged with words or discussed with others.

You can take this approach with all the fairies illustrated in the cards, though it is inadvisable to work with those inimical to humans, such as the Boggart. Begin by meditating on the fairy and the situation depicted in the card, then transfer the knowledge gained to your own locality, where the spirits may appear quite differently. To contact the local water fairy, sit by a stream or lake and meditate. To contact the spirits of the local forest, meditate beneath the trees. You may have to observe some fairies silently, others may talk with you and share their knowledge, and others you would be foolish to approach at all.

If you are serious about working with fairy energies, remember that they must all be treated with the greatest respect, and, above all, heed this decree:

> *To Will*
> *To Know*
> *To Dare*
> *And to Keep Silence.*

The Spring Court

₳CE

₳RÍEL

The Card: The card shows a tall, ethereal, male fairy wearing floating, yellow draperies. A hawk accompanies him as he flies in the air.

The Fairy: In occult lore, the fairy Ariel is an air elemental. Shakespeare mentioned him in *The Tempest*, saying that with his song, he could bind or loose the winds, enchant men or drive them mad.

Elementals are spirits living in or composed entirely of one of the ancient elements of earth, air, fire, or water. The sixteenth-century magician Paracelsus named the spirits of the air *sylphs* and added that they are kindly disposed toward humankind.[1] Sylphs usually live high in the mountain peaks. Sometimes their voices are heard on the wind or their airy forms are felt in passing, though they are rarely seen. They are described as almost transparent, very small, and winged, or alternatively as tall with long, feathered wings, large, hawklike eyes, and angular faces.

The term *sylph* is derived from the Greek word *silphe*, which means a "butterfly" or "moth"—indeed, fairies are popularly depicted with butterfly wings. The ancient Celts regarded butterflies as symbols of fairies or ancestral spirits (often considered to be one and the same), and they appear in Celtic stories as guides to the Otherworld or Fairyland, where the dead also dwelled.

Ariel is an air elemental and controls all the powers of air. His winds circle the earth. Inhaled air is the sustaining breath of life; exhaled air carries the words, poetry, and songs that communicate human ideas and knowledge. But words can wound as well as praise, condemn as well as exalt. The gentle summer breeze can become the destructive hurricane. It is for this reason that the magical symbol of air is a double-edged sword.

Divinatory Meanings: Ariel flies into the cards today to herald a completely new phase in the questioner's life. Ariel arrives on the wind of change. The questioner's ideas and opinions will be revolutionized. It is a fortuitous time for formal study, developing new ideas, communicating ideas, writing, or performing.

Reversed Meanings: When Ariel appears reversed in the cards, he indicates muddled thinking, rigid but mistaken ideas, and a period of disagreements, conflicts, and quarrels.

Working with a Sylph: Sylphs rule the element of air. In magic, air is concerned with thought, ideas, and communication. If you need to work on these areas of your life, you might request the aid of the air elementals.

Prepare an incense of air by mixing one teaspoon dried lavender, two teaspoons benzoin resin, two teaspoons acacia resin, two teaspoons white sandalwood, and a few drops of lemon verbena oil.[2] Burn a pinch or two of this on a charcoal block (available at church and occult stores). Magically, the rising of the incense smoke represents the element of air. This incense attracts air elementals.

Say, "Ye Lords of Air, I implore you to come to me, and to aid me in my work." Close your eyes and relax, ready to take a journey in your imagination.

The sun is rising over a spring meadow, and a warm breeze stirs the flowers. Through the clouds, blown on the wind, the elemental of the air appears before you. Take note of his appearance and tell him your name. If you wish, you can ask for help with your mental abilities, intellectual matters of concentration, or your imagination, memory, and clarity of mind. When you are ready to return, thank the elemental, and return yourself to waking consciousness.

Two

LEPRECHAUN

The Card: A small man, dressed in green, works at his cobbler's last, making a single shoe. His ears are pointed, and his face is wrinkled, but it is friendly and jolly. He sits at the edge of a field just greening with spring corn. There is a rainbow in the sky, at the end of which the leprechaun's pot of gold is hidden from sight, no doubt!

The Fairy: Leprechauns are famous fairy cobblers who make all the shoes for the fairy gentry, though they are always seen working on a single shoe, never a pair.[3] In appearance, leprechauns are small, withered, and dressed in a homely fashion, in shabby, green frockcoats. They carry shillelaghs and are often seen smoking pipes. They live in isolated places, under the hedgerows or in gullies. They are solitary beings who rarely associate with other fairies. Some say that they are the products of unions between humans and the Sidhe.

Leprechaun is really only the Leinster name for them, and they have different names in other parts of Ireland. They are called Cluricane in County Cork, Luricane in Kerry, Lurigadaune in Tipperary, and Loghery-man in Ulster.[4]

Leprechauns own all the underground riches of Ireland. They always have pots of gold hidden at the end of the rainbow, but hate to part with it. There is an old tale of a boy from Castlerea who dearly loved books and wanted to find a pot of money with which to buy more. One evening he discovered a leprechaun under a dock leaf and grabbed him with the intent of appropriating his treasure. The leprechaun said that there was no need for violence, as they were cousins once removed; the boy was a changeling and only those with fairy blood could possess the gold.

The leprechaun took the boy to the old fort of Lipenshaw and led him through a secret door in the stone wall. The floor of the room inside was covered in gold pieces. The fairy told the boy, "Take what you want, but when the last glow of the sun vanishes, the gold will also vanish." The lad loaded his pockets with as much gold as he could carry, and was just going back for more when the door shut. He put the money in a bank in Dublin and became very rich and learned.[5]

Divinatory Meanings: When the Leprechaun appears in your cards, he indicates material gain in the form of lottery or gambling winnings, competition prizes, gifts, legacies, or some other unexpected windfall. Whether the leprechaun's gift is large or small, you must be careful how you use it, otherwise it may lose its charms, or disappear as fast as the fairy gold that turns to dust and withered leaves when the sun rises!

Reversed Meanings: If the Leprechaun appears reversed in your spread today, prepare to seize unexpected opportunities. These could involve a career change, the chance to travel, or interesting new friendships. Success comes from learning new skills.

Working with a Leprechaun: It is most likely that the term *leprechaun* is derived from *Lugh-chromain*, which means "little stooping Lugh," and that the leprechaun is a diminutive form of the old god Lugh.[6] After the harvest, Lugh was identified with the god Crom Dubh, the "dark croucher" or the "old bent one" who dwelled in the fairy mounds.

Legends tell us that the leprechaun keeps a pot of gold hidden at the end of the rainbow. This treasure might be the precious metals of the earth, or it might symbolize the light of the summer sun, the yellow grain of the harvest, or riches of the spirit. If you have ever tried to stand at the end of a rainbow, you will know that it is a place that cannot be reached physically, but only in spirit. For this reason, the rainbow is often thought to be the bridge to the world of the gods—the afterlife, or Fairyland.

The comical depictions of leprechauns in popular culture should not blind us to the fact that they are ancient spirits whose stories have persisted down the centuries. Approach them with respect.

THREE

BROWNIE

The Card: The card shows a homely female brownie, clad in a brown pinafore, sweeping the hearth of a cottage with a besom.

The Fairy: Brownies are solitary fairies found in southern Scotland and the northern counties of England. They become attached to particular houses or families, and while the humans are asleep, they work about the house or farm, cleaning, tidying up, or helping with the brewing. When the cock crows, the brownie knows it is time to go to bed. The only reward they ask is a bowl of cream or fresh milk.

Brownies are very good at hiding and can make themselves disappear at will, but those who have seen them describe them as small, shaggy-haired, and ugly, with flat faces. They are often ragged in appearance, but they are offended by gifts of clothes and will promptly disappear forever if given a new suit; so if you have a helpful house fairy, don't be tempted to reward it in this fashion.

Brownies have a mischievous side and like to play tricks on humans, such as rattling the fire irons, smashing crockery, hiding objects, or making a mess. They are easily offended, and if they are mistreated, they turn into destructive boggarts.

Belief in house spirits is ancient. It was once the custom to make gifts to such a spirit before entering a dwelling, offering it bread and salt.[7] In ancient Rome, this spirit was called the *lar familiaris* ("household lar") and was given daily offerings of food and monthly gifts of garlands, all placed on the hearth shrine. The lar protected the house and its wealth. Its presence was invoked on family occasions such as birthdays, weddings, births, and deaths.

Though some Victorian writers claimed that the concept of household spirits may have spread with the Roman Empire, there is enough evidence to prove that the belief in such spirits evolved independently in places as far apart as China, western Europe, and South America. Today, this is generally reduced to the notion of a good or bad atmosphere in a house.

Divinatory Meanings: When the Brownie appears in your cards, she is telling you that pleasure and fulfillment will come from your home and family. They are your security, the important bedrock on which you build the rest of your life, and the refuge from the vicissitudes of the world to which you return. Here lies true happiness. There may be family parties and celebrations in the offing, perhaps a reunion.

Reversed Meanings: When the Brownie appears reversed in your cards, you will be recognized and admired by those outside of your home and family. Your efforts and talents will be rewarded.

Working with a Brownie: To attract and honor a brownie, make an altar in a small wall niche or on the mantle shelf over the fireplace, since this is the traditional shrine of the house spirit. Place on it an image that represents the spirit, or something that you associate with the sanctity and work of the home. Place regular offerings of flowers on the altar, especially at family gatherings and occasions. Tell the fairy all the family news. Never make demands, and place offerings on the altar instead of saying "thank you," which brownies don't like.

Four
BÉFÍND

The Card: The card shows a cradle in which a baby lies. Appearing behind it are three fairies, the foremost of which is Béfind. She holds a spindle, while her two companions hold a measuring rod and shears.

The Fairy: Béfind is an Irish fairy godmother. Her name simply means "white lady," a title given to many female fairies. Along with two other spirits, she appears at the birth of a child to predict its future and to bestow fairy gifts upon it.

Stories of fairy godmothers are familiar to everyone. We all know the tale of Sleeping Beauty, in which kind fairies blessed the baby princess with gifts such as beauty and a sweet nature, while a single jealous fairy cursed the girl with eternal sleep, should she ever prick her finger on a spinning wheel. Not so long ago, people all over Europe believed that fairy godmothers would arrive when a child was born to determine its future, blessing it or cursing it according to the behavior of the family and the welcome extended to the spirits.

Belief in these figures is very ancient, having its origin in the worship of ancient goddesses of fate such as the Three Fates, or the Three Norns, who span the thread of life, wove its pattern, and cut the thread at death. The word *fairy* is probably derived from the Latin word for fate, *fata*, via the Old French *fee*. According to Greek myth, the Three Fates, or *Moerae*, control human destiny. Their Greek name means "phase," as in the phases of the moon, and they are in fact a manifestation of the triple moon goddess, the spinner and measurer of time, as it waxes to full and then wanes. The thread of life is spun on Clotho's spindle, measured by the rod of Lachesis, and snipped by Atropos' shears. In stature, Atropos is the smallest of the three, but by far the most feared, since she is the death goddess.

Fairy godmothers appear three times in a person's life: at birth, at marriage, and at death, when they lead the soul into the Otherworld.

Divinatory Meanings: When Béfind appears in a spread, she indicates some kind of rite of passage, since she manifests at births, marriages, and deaths. The surrounding cards may reveal which of these events is indicated, though the card may simply herald a life-changing experience for the questioner.

Reversed Meanings: If Béfind appears reversed in a spread, she is advising you that you are not using the gifts you are blessed with. These gifts have been bestowed for a purpose, and fulfillment will come from using them. Rejoice in who and what you truly are, rather than what others wish you to be.

Working with a Béfind: If you are expecting a baby and wish to earn the blessing of the fairy godmothers, you should prepare the house to welcome them. It should be cleaned, thoroughly swept, and kept quiet and orderly. On the day of the birth, the table should be laid with honey, bread, and three white almonds. Coins and gifts for the new baby can be placed beside the food. A light should be left burning in the house, so that the fairies can find their way. Since most babies are born in a hospital, this little ceremony can be carried out when the baby is first brought home.

FIVE

FAIRY HART/UNICORN

The Card: The upright card shows a white hart with golden hooves, while reflected in the pool is an ethereal unicorn.

The Fairy: The white hart, or fairy deer, often appears in old stories, sparking off a chase or series of events that involves the hero in a spiritual quest. The deer was one of the four sacred animals of the Celts and has played an important role in folklore in many parts of the world. Stags, especially white ones, are frequently mentioned in ancient Celtic myth as fairy animals who entice heroes to the Otherworld. One hart led King Arthur through a cave to Morgan le Fay's Fairyland palace, where he was shown the heavens and the earth. In Irish mythology, Oisin was the son of the deer goddess Sadb and, near the end of his life, saw a vision in which a hornless fawn was pursued over the waters of the sea by the red and white hounds of the Underworld. The fawn was Oisin himself. In Welsh myth, Pwyll, Prince of Dyfed, chanced to meet Arawn, Lord of the Underworld, hunting a stag, and was asked to temporarily become Lord of the Dead himself. The stag Arawn was hunting was, in fact, Pwyll's own soul.

• • •

The unicorn is a magical beast that dwells in Fairyland and is seldom seen by humans, though humans all over the world have known about unicorns. The first written record comes from Ctesis of Cnidos, a Greek historian and physician, and dates from 398 B.C.E. He wrote a book on India saying that there were certain wild asses that were as large as horses, or even larger. Their bodies were white, their heads dark red, and their eyes dark blue. They had a horn on the forehead that was about a foot and a half in length, the base of which was pure white, the middle portion black, and the upper part sharp and colored a vivid crimson.

For many, the unicorn is a symbol of purity, of the soul within the dark matter of material form, and the perfect reconciliation of opposites. In heraldry, the unicorn is a symbol of "the very parfit gentil knight." According to the bestiaries of the Middle Ages, the unicorn was too fierce and fleet to be caught by hunters. It could only be captured by a virgin, being attracted by her virtue. In one tale, the virgin sits beneath a tree to lure the unicorn. It lays its head in her lap and permits itself to be caressed to sleep. She then breaks its horn, the hunters pounce, and the unicorn is secured and taken to the palace of the king. (This appears to be a story of betrayal, but is perhaps a sexual allegory.)

The unicorn's horn is called an alicorn and is reputed to be an antidote to poison. Once, a great lake was poisoned by the venom of a serpent, until a unicorn approached and passed his horn over it. Several Renaissance lords claimed that they possessed unicorn horn cups, and these were frequently on display at banquets as a defense against death by poisoning—a real threat when invited to dine in some court circles. The horn was said to sweat in the presence of poison. Alicorns were bought and sold at fabulous prices and were among the most precious possessions of princes and popes. The poor were sold water into which the horn had been dipped. It was even believed that an alicorn could raise the dead. However, some say that the horn is a cone of light arising from the unicorn's third eye center.

Divinatory Meanings: When the Fairy Hart appears in your cards, it challenges you to follow, wherever it may lead. Though this may sometimes be difficult and unpleasant, it will engender changes that prove beneficial in the end. You will develop and grow immeasurably if you meet the challenge with courage and determination. The white hart is a messenger from the Higher Realms, calling on you to pursue your life quest.

Reversed Meanings: Where the unicorn treads, a great blessing follows. He brings gentle healing from the Otherworld. He is the harbinger of hope, relief from anxieties, spiritual inspiration, and true joy.

Working with the Fairy Hart: You can meet the fairy hart in your imagination whenever you need its help. Relax and imagine yourself in a clearing amid a deep forest. A dappled light shines through the tree canopy. All is still, apart from the joyful song of various birds. Then into the clearing steps a magnificent white hart. It looks calmly at you for a moment or two, and you realize that this is no mortal creature, but a fairy beast. It turns, seemingly asking you to follow it.

You chase through the forest in the wake of the hart, feeling strong and wild and full of vigor. The path twists and turns, and you begin to notice that objects and shapes appear beside the path, or sometimes as obstacles on it. Take note of these, because they are important and represent those things in your life that may help or hinder you.

The hart may lead you further on to show you the heart of the forest, or it may stop, having shown you all that is necessary for the present. When you are ready to leave, thank the stag, and return yourself to waking consciousness.

Working with the Unicorn: Relax. Imagine that you are in a woodland clearing, standing beside a still, clear pool. It is warm and sunny, and you feel relaxed and comfortable. Water trickles into the pool over mossy rocks, and you notice a golden cup attached to the rocks by a silver chain. You are thirsty but feel that to drink from this cup without an invitation would be wrong.

Suddenly the air seems to shimmer and the forest hushes. A resplendent, stately, white unicorn appears before you. You feel purity and nobility radiating from it. After a while it steps toward the pool, dipping its silver horn into the water. The water glistens and seems filled with a soft light. Stepping back, the unicorn invites you to drink.

You dip the golden cup into the water and drink deeply. It is cool and sweet and fills you with energy. It is the water of healing, of renewal. Feel its force enter into you.

When you are ready to leave, bow to the unicorn. Gradually bring yourself back to waking consciousness.

SIX

GARCONER

The Card: The card shows a handsome, Gypsy-looking elf, wearing a red coat and a yellow neckerchief. His hair is black and curly, and he has a twinkle in his eye and an invitation in his glance. In the background is a tinker's cart and caravan.

The Fairy: Garconer is an Irish elf who looks like a handsome Gypsy, with bright, black eyes and dark, curly hair. His name means "love talker," and he loves to seduce mortal women, but beware! Any woman who yields to his sweet words and kisses is lost; she will pine away and die when he leaves—and he always does leave.

Fairies take a romantic interest in human men and women. Fairy men sometimes appear as strangers at village dances to make love to pretty girls. These girls will never be the same again, wasting away with longing for their absent fairy lovers. Fairy kings take women to their underground palaces, but return them seven years later, prematurely old and worn-out from the demands of their fairy husbands.

Beautiful fairy women may call to men from the depths of the forest. Once a man has been held in the arms of his fairy sweetheart, he is her slave; she will draw his life from him, growing stronger and stronger as he grows paler and weaker. Some fairy women even suck the blood of their lovers. Water fairies and mermaids, in particular, long for human men. They appear on the banks of a lake or the sea, seductively combing their golden hair. Should a man reach out to the lovely fairy, she will seize him and drag him beneath the waves, drowning him and stealing his soul to keep in a lobster pot.

Sometimes, though, the marriage of a fairy and a human can work out, so long as the human does not break any of the taboos imposed on the relationship. These might include a man not being able to see his fairy wife on a certain day, never touching her with iron, and certainly never striking her. If he does any of these things, she will assuredly be off, back to the land of the fairy, taking her dowry with her. Children of these marriages will be passionate and fey, possessing marvelous gifts for poetry, music, or the second sight.

Divinatory Meanings: The appearance of the "Love Talker" indicates possible attractions and new relationships. Depending on surrounding cards, this card may imply temptation or instant gratification at the expense of long-term happiness.

Reversed Meanings: If Garconer is reversed in your spread, his message is that you are ignoring your present circumstances and opportunities to live in the past, dwelling on old loves and glories, and wallowing in nostalgia.

Working with a Fairy Love: Not recommended.

SEVEN

ASRAI

The Card: The card shows a delicate, young water fairy at the edge of a pool in the twilight. She reaches toward a dragonfly. In the foreground are blue irises.

The Fairy: Asrai are small and dainty water fairies found in the west of England. They melt into a pool of water when captured or exposed to sunlight, as the following story shows:

A certain fisherman was out on the lake one night. He had no luck for many hours, but as the moon emerged from the clouds, his net grew heavy. When he hauled it into the bottom of his boat, he saw that he had caught an asrai in his net: a lovely, gentle water fairy. He knew that these fairies only rose from their deep homes below the water once every hundred years, so although this one only looked like a twelve-year-old girl, he thought it must be very old.

He began to think that he would like to show the creature to his children—how it would delight them! And perhaps the rich folk at the castle would pay to display it in their ornamental pond? He certainly needed the money. Hardening his heart to the pitiful pleadings of the fairy, he began to row toward the shore. The distraught creature managed to free an arm from the net and pointed at the moon as if to beg for her freedom. She laid a hand on the fisherman's arm, and it felt like cool foam, but it seemed that the man's warmth hurt the asrai and she quickly withdrew it. Moreover, the dawn was approaching and she seemed to flinch from the light, huddling down in the bottom of the boat and trying to cover herself with her long, green hair. The fisherman took pity and laid wet rushes over her.

The lake was long and the sun had risen by the time he reached his creek. Wearily he drew the boat ashore and lifted the rushes to gloat over his prize, but his net was empty! All that remained was a damp patch in the bottom of the boat. But the arm the fairy had touched was icy cold for the rest of his life, and nothing could warm it.[8]

Divinatory Meanings: When the fragile Asrai appears in your cards, she indicates some kind of moral choice, perhaps simply between right and wrong, or perhaps between the spiritual and the material. Listen to your conscience. Any choice should be carefully examined and its repercussions considered. You might greedily grasp what appears to be a glittering prize, only to have it turn to ashes in your hands.

Reversed Meanings: The Asrai reversed indicates the abandonment of the spiritual for the purely material, and the wish to gain wealth, whatever the cost. She warns that selfish behavior will have to be paid for.

Working with a Water Fairy: In ancient times, the spirits of life-sustaining water were honored. Offerings were cast into rivers and lakes: coins, jewelery, pins, and ritual weapons. Even today, we throw coins into wishing wells to solicit good luck from its resident nymph. Our ancestors knew that all rivers, lakes, and streams were sacred. But before you start throwing bits of metal into waterways, reflect on the environmental impact (it is also illegal in many places); you can offer flowers, but the spirit might be more pleased if you did it a good service by cleaning up trash thrown into the water and avoiding polluting it yourself.

EIGHT

BILLY WINKER

The Card: The card shows a grinning male fairy clad in a night-cap and gown, holding a candlestick. He creeps through a blue bedroom.

The Fairy: Billy Winker is a fairy from Lancashire, in the north of England. He appears at bedtime to bring sleep to children.

Billy is just one manifestation of a sleep fairy, and there are many others all over the world. They include the Sandman, who sprinkles magic dust in the eyes of children to make them sleep, the Dutch Klaas Vaak, the French La Dormette, and the Danish Old Luk Oie. The Scottish name for Billy Winker is Wee Willie Winky, immortalized in this nursery rhyme:

Wee Willie Winky runs through the town,
Upstairs and downstairs in his night gown
Rapping at the windows,
Tapping at the lock
"Are the children all in bed?
For now it's eight o'clock!"

The power to bring sleep is one of the great fairy magics. The Irish fairy Aillen mac Midhna traveled to the court of the High King in Tara, where his magical music lulled all the inhabitants to sleep, and he was able to destroy the castle with three fiery breaths. Also in Celtic myth, the god Angus and the swan maiden Caer Ibormeith circled Loch Bel Dracon three times, singing a magical song that put everyone in the vicinity to sleep for three days, while Cascorach, the minstrel of the Tuatha dé Danaan, lured St. Patrick to sleep with his music.

Fairies seem to be associated with sleep, perhaps because one of the entrances to Fairyland is through dreams. Any human sleeping in some fairy-haunted place, such as an ancient mound, stone circle, dolmen, or solitary hawthorn, may be taken away to the Otherworld.

Divinatory Meanings: When Billy Winker appears in your cards, he heralds recuperation, convalescence from an illness, or the end of some trouble that has been worrying you. He indicates a period of rest and relaxation, perhaps a holiday.

Reversed Meanings: Billy Winker reversed in your cards is warning you that self-indulgence will lead to difficulties that take longer to cure than create. He may indicate problems relating to overindulgence, smoking, or drinking.

Working with a Sleep Fairy: Fairies don't like to see themselves in mirrors, so if you want to attract a sleep fairy into your bedroom, you must remove these. (According to the precepts of feng shui, mirrors create energy disturbances when they face a bed, so perhaps the fairies know something we don't!) You can attract a spirit of sleep with a few drops of lavender or camomile oil on your pillow, or dried hop flowers made into a little pillow to place on top of your own.

NÍNE

PÍXÍE

The Card: The card shows a tiny, green pixie holding a staff. In the background is an old, stone quoit (an ancient burial chamber).

The Fairy: Pixies are little green fairies that are only found in the southwest of England, though they are generally called piskies in Cornwall. Large bands of them can be found on the wild heath of Dartmoor, as can be discerned from the number of places named after them there, including Pixie's Holt, Pixie's Cave, and Pixie's Parlour. At night they mount the wild Dartmoor ponies and ride them madly through the night, twisting and knotting their manes.

Pixies are full of mischief and love to play practical jokes. Many travelers have set off across the moor and found themselves hopelessly lost when the fairies bewitched the path. This is called being "pixy-led," and the only remedy is to turn your coat inside out, as this will confuse them long enough for you to get away.

However, pixies are not malicious creatures and have been known to help those in need. If a farmer treats them with respect, they might finish his work for him while he sleeps, doing chores about the house and yard, especially the threshing of the grain.[9] But be warned. If you have helpful pixies, don't make them a gift of new clothes. One kindly farmer noticed that his accommodating pixie wore tattered clothes and had his wife make him a new suit. The pixie delightedly put on his new outfit and disappeared, never to be seen again.

Divinatory Meanings: You have been going through a difficult time, but the playful pixies are asking you to stop taking everything so seriously, lighten up, and have some fun! Laughter can be a great antidote to the trials of life. There is much truth in the saying "Laughter is the best medicine"; it really does reduce stress levels and boost the immune system. Remember when you were a child and the world was a wondrous and exciting place? Try to recover a little of this feeling.

Reversed Meanings: You are shirking some task or responsibility. At the moment, you don't care about hurting others as long as you get what you want. This attitude will have consequences for you at a later date.

Working with a Pixie: You can visit the realm of the pixies in your imagination.

Relax. Imagine that you are standing in the middle of Dartmoor. The heathland is wild and lonely, covered in heather and wind-twisted shrubs. A few shaggy, wild ponies graze the vegetation.

Gradually you become aware of the sound of laughter and the tinkling of tiny bells. It is coming from a large, strangely shaped rock that lies a few yards away. Cautiously you start to walk toward the sound, and the giggling becomes louder.

Suddenly a little green man steps around the rock, followed by half a dozen more. They skip and frolic about your feet, their faces lit with glee. Their gaiety is infectious. You find yourself laughing, too. These creatures are incapable of taking anything seriously.

They may show you the pixie mound where they live, or take you for a wild ride across the heath on a little Dartmoor pony. Spend as much time with these merry creatures as you wish. When you leave, you will bring some of their joy back with you. This is the lesson of the pixies—they exude a natural, childlike delight in life.

When you are ready to leave, thank the pixies, and return to waking consciousness.

THE WHITE LADY

THE LADY OF THE SPRING COURT
THE WHITE LADY

The Card: The card depicts a lovely, pale woman with flowing, silver hair. She floats over a mountainous ravine in which a waterfall crashes down the rocks. The air is eerie and misty blue.

The Fairy: White ladies are common in fairy lore. Sometimes the name of a fairy will simply mean "white lady," as with the African Shamantin and the Irish Béfind. They usually haunt particular locations, usually wild, unspoiled places such as ravines, waterfalls, mountain ridges, and virgin forests. Sometimes they are the guardians of natural fountains and springs.

The White Lady is a *genius loci*—a being that protects or embodies the soul of a specific place. The ancients believed that spirits were attached to various trees, streams, rocks, and other natural features, but not all rocks, trees, and features. Those inhabited by a spirit might appear slightly odd or unusual, or have different plant growth in the vicinity, or animals might act strangely in the area. This spirit might appear spontaneously to favored humans, and there are many legends concerning them all over the world. Our ancestors marked out any place where such a spirit appeared as a sacred place, and treated it with reverence.[10]

Two white ladies appear in the Arthurian myths. The name of Queen Guinevere means "white phantom" (*Gwenhwyvar*). She was a flower bride, married in May, and represents the protective spirit of the land of Albion (Britain). The other is Morgan (*Mor Gwyn* = "white lady") le Fay, Arthur's sister, the protective spirit of the Otherworld, the island of Avalon.

Divinatory Meanings: The White Lady indicates that a visit to a special place, or a particular event, will lead to great changes in your thinking and way of life. It may not seem significant when it happens, but it is a tiny seed planted in your subconsciousness, and from little acorns mighty oaks may grow!

The White Lady may betoken a real person in your life: an attractive girl or young woman who is fun-loving, convivial, and adventurous. She can be a very loyal and warm friend, but is easily hurt. Upset her and you will make a bad enemy.

Reversed Meanings: The White Lady reversed indicates that you are ungrounded and have a feeling of being rootless and adrift, not knowing which direction to take.

The reversed card may represent a real person in your life: a shallow, superficial young woman who only cares about herself. She may seem to be a friend, but she is using you for her own ends.

Working with a White Lady: Traditional witches and shamans always try to contact place-spirits when seeking a sacred place to work, recognizing that real magic grows out of a spiritual connection with the land. Without this, ritual can be a barren, intellectual conceit.

Such a connection can only be achieved by quiet meditation in your chosen spot. Go there without asking anything, and visit it frequently until its guardian spirit makes itself known. It may welcome you and your magical activities, or it may tell you to leave, in which case you must obey.

THE KNAVE OF THE SPRING COURT
TIDDY MUN

The Card: The card shows a drably clad fairy with white hair and a long, white beard. He is running through the reeds of the misty fenland of East Anglia. A windmill is in the background.

The Fairy: A Tiddy Mun ("little man") is a yarthkin, a water fairy living in the Fens of the eastern counties of England, a region that largely lay under water until drains and ditches were put in. The countryside is still dotted with the old windmills that pumped the water. Its human inhabitants were thought to be strange and webfooted themselves, but they feared the marsh fairies and, going out at darkling every night bearing lights in their hands, circled around their houses chanting charms to keep them away. A Tiddy Mun can summon the mists, call up disease from the marshes, and control the water. The old fenmen would appeal to the yarthkins to calm the floodwaters:

> *"Tiddy Mun wi'out a name*
> *Tha watters thruff!"*

If they heard a noise like a peewit, they knew that the Tiddy Mun had heard them and would answer their pleas. Yarthkins are also connected with fertility. Offerings of bread and salt were placed on flat stones to solicit a good harvest.[11]

A Tiddy Mun lives in the green water holes and comes out in the evenings when the mists rise into the twilight. He limps along like an old man, and has long, white hair and a long, white beard, all matted and tangled, and wears a long, drab gown that hides him in the mist or dusk. He whistles like the wind and laughs like a peewit.

The Tiddy Mun is thought to be better natured than most of the local fairies and often helps people, but he can be dangerous when angered. When the fens were drained, the Tiddy Muns became so angry that they brought pestilence on both children and cattle until they were pacified with offerings and prayers.[12]

One particularly nasty yarthkin, called Yallery Brown ("Yellowy Brown"), was once discovered by a man who found it moaning piteously beneath a stone, all cocooned in its own yellow hair. It offered him gifts in return for freeing it.[13] The man had cause to regret his kindness, however, for Yallery Brown was the most evil thing that ever lived. All the help the man received caused more harm than good.

Divinatory Meanings: When the kindly Tiddy Mun appears, he heralds success, though not of a material nature, and satisfaction in a job well done. He represents a helpful friend and innocent pleasures.

Tiddy Mun may represent a real person in your life: a charming young man who is romantic and idealistic, with old-fashioned ideas of chivalry and gentleness.

Reversed Meanings: The Tiddy Mun reversed warns that you may be trying to ignore an unpleasant situation. He indicates cruelty and ingratitude, and perhaps an enemy made.

He may represent a real person in the life of the questioner: a dishonest, selfish young man who is cruel and deceitful.

Working with the Tiddy Mun: If you live in a boggy or swampy place, or near water, you can honor the local spirits in the manner of the old Fenmen. Place a flat stone in the garden on which little offerings can be placed. These can be flowers, pretty stones or shells, bread, and salt.

QUEEN

THE SEA MITHER

THE QUEEN OF THE SPRING COURT
THE SEA MITHER

The Card: The card shows a beautiful, motherly woman rising from the gentle ocean waves. She is dressed and cloaked in sea blue, and a circlet of rare dark pearls is on her forehead. She holds a cornucopia from which she pours shining silver fish into the water.

The Fairy: This benevolent fairy appears in the lore of the Orkney Isles, which lie off the northernmost coast of Scotland. In the summer, the Sea Mither (mother) brings warmth and seasonal calm to the island waters. Under her rule, life and summer return to the sea and to the islands. She brings the shoals of fish to the sea and the blossoms to the earth, and under her rule animals mate and breed.

The winter is ruled by her archenemy Teran, who stirs up the sea and sky to cause the rough winter weather. He causes havoc on both sea and land, whipping up storms, bringing ice and cold, and drowning the fishermen. Lying at the bottom of the ocean, the grieving Sea Mither hears their cries and longs for spring, when she will rule once more.

Every spring, at the equinox, the Sea Mither begins to battle with Teran to bring in the summer. At the end of the fight, which may go on for weeks, he is bound and imprisoned at the bottom of the sea. At the autumn equinox, Teran escapes and they fight once again. This time Teran is victorious and the Sea Mither is banished.

Fairies often personify the weather or the seasons. In Scottish lore, the Cailleach is the winter. Just as she is the folklore survival of the ancient crone goddess, the Sea Mither is a manifestation of the mother goddess. Ancient humans personified the earth and the sea as mother goddesses, since they "give birth" to all the life that exists in the world, and nurture it with their bounty. The Sea Mither is the patroness of fertility. She provides the vegetation, sends the rain, creates the animals, brings forth the fish, and presides over love, marriage, and childbirth.

Divinatory Meanings: When the Sea Mither appears in your cards, powerful creative energies surround you, indicating fertility, abundance, stability, partnerships, a happy marriage, and perhaps the creation of works of art, music, or literature. Sometimes she may herald the birth of a child.

Her appearance in the cards may indicate a real woman in the questioner's life: a graceful woman who is intelligent, artistic, honest, and generous.

Reversed Meanings: The Sea Mither reversed indicates poverty, lack, sterility, blocked creativity, or domestic upheaval. Sometimes the card may mean a desperate promiscuity born of loneliness and the need to be loved.

The Sea Mither reversed may refer to a real woman, perhaps a widow or lonely woman, who is a bitter and malicious gossip.

Working with the Sea Mither: You can encounter the Sea Mother in the following pathworking:

Relax. Imagine that you are walking beside the seashore on a fine spring morning. Though the weather has been stormy, the skies are clearing and the sun is out.

You gaze far out across the sea and feel that something wonderful is about to happen. Then suddenly, only a few feet away from you, a beautiful woman rises from the waves. She is dressed in sea blue, and a string of black pearls circles her forehead. She is the Sea Mother who brings the summer and returns life to the land and sea.

In her arms she bears a shell, from which she pours shining silver fish into the sea. Now the fishermen will have full nets again.

She wades ashore and smiles as she passes you, going into the orchards. From the shell she pours seed onto the ground, and sweet spring grass rises from the moist, brown earth. Now the animals will have full bellies again. As she passes, the fruit trees blossom, and flowers grow where she has stepped. Now the farmers will have full barns and baskets.

Enchanted, you follow her, and when she has finished her work, she turns to you and asks what gift you would like. Think carefully about this, as your reply might please or anger her. If she thinks it right, she may grant your wish.

When you are ready to leave, allow the scene to fade around you, and return yourself to waking consciousness.

THE KING OF THE SPRING COURT

THE WOODWOSE

The Card: The card shows a fairy wildman with long, unkempt hair and a beard. He strides ferociously through the woodlands, wielding a great club.

The Fairy: A woodwose is a forest spirit, sometimes also called a wildman or a woodwouse. Woodwoses have a shaggy appearance and are often naked and covered only in their own hair. They do not seem to speak. They are powerful, pre-Celtic spirits of the forest, hiding from human contact.

Some woodwoses were originally human. Merlin spent time as a wildman, or Merlin Wyllt—the Wild Merlin.[14] He fled into the forest after losing a battle, insane with grief. He lost his humanity and became one of the strange woodland creatures who rampaged in crazed rapture through the greenwood, living like beasts with their hair and beards grown long and matted. It was there that he learned the deep truths of the shaman, living between madness and ecstasy. There he became the accomplished seer and magician we recognize. Sir Lancelot also spent time as a wildman after losing his wits, and Sir Perceval was a wildman before going to Camelot to become a knight.

Nearly three hundred European coats of arms contain a depiction of a woodwose. The coat of arms of the Earls of Atholl in Scotland features a wildman in shackles. It is explained that one of their ancestors captured a wildman by giving him athollbrose (honey and whisky) to drink.

The wildman was once a well-known figure, represented at pageants and parades. When Queen Elizabeth I visited Kenilworth Castle, she was greeted by a man dressed as a woodwose, bearing an oak sapling.

The wildman is connected with the Green Man, who personified the life of the vegetation spirits. In Britain this spirit of vegetation is still portrayed on May Day by the Green Man, Jack in the Bush, or Jack in the Green, in the guise of a mummer clad in green leaves and fresh boughs. He is also depicted on many pub signs and church carvings as a head with shoots and leaves growing from the mouth.

Divinatory Meanings: The Woodwose represents the call of the wild and the original, leaving behind the known for the unknown. He is a breath of fresh air, and indicates the rejection of established values, and normal life overturned. However, there is a sense of optimism in the air, notwithstanding unexpected events and circumstances.

The card may indicate a real person in the life of the questioner: a mature man who is lively, energetic, and noble, but unorthodox and unconventional—a man who throws everything around him into chaos.

Reversed Meanings: The Woodwose reversed indicates reckless or impulsive behavior, a waste of energy and the frittering away of talent, an unwillingness to give way or compromise, or wrongly directed anger and rage.

The reversed card may indicate a real person in the life of the questioner: an intolerant man who is stubborn and prejudiced. He is probably a person who starts many things, but finishes nothing.

Working with a Wildman: If you want to know the wildman, you must discover the wild part of yourself. His is the magic of dance, drumming, ecstatic vision, assimilating the animal part of your nature, moving beyond the mundane, and exploring beyond your limits.

The story of Merlin as a wildman parallels descriptions of shamanic experience from many parts of the world. Merlin learned to access the wild, instinctive, animal part of his own nature; to let go of the logical, critical side in order to be able to achieve visions and access the Otherworld.

1. Paracelsus (1493–1541), in his *Treatise on Elemental Sprites*.

2. If you don't have all of these, you could just use one of them, or evaporate some lavender oil or lemon verbena oil. You could also just crush some mint leaves and inhale the scent.

3. Lady Wilde, *Ancient Legends, Mystic Charms and Superstitions of Ireland* (London: Ward & Downey, 1887).

4. Crofton Croker, *Fairy Legends and Traditions of the South of Ireland* (London: John Murray, 1826).

5. Lady Wilde, ibid.

6. Peter Berresford Ellis, *Dictionary of Celtic Mythology* (London: Constable & Co., Ltd., 1992).

7. Eric Maple, "The House," *Man, Myth and Magic*.

8. Adapted from Ruth Tongue, *Forgotten Folk-Tales of the English Counties* (London: Routledge & Kegan Paul, 1970).

9. Robert Hunt, *Popular Romances of the West of England* (1881; reprint, London: Chatto and Windus, 1930).

10. Nigel Pennick, *Natural Magic* (London: Thorsons, 2001).

11. M. C. Balfour, *Legends of the Cars* (London: Folk-Lore II, 1891).

12. Ibid.

13. Ibid.

14. Bob Curran, *Creatures of Celtic Myth* (London: Cassell & Co., 2000).

The Summer Court

ACE

THE FIRE DRAKE

The Card: The picture shows a hearth fire blazing in the grate. Horse brasses are hung on the fireplace for luck, and candles burn on the mantlepiece. A small dragon, called a fire drake, basks in the warmth.

The Fairy: In Celtic and Germanic lore, fire drakes are dragon-like creatures with sinuous necks, bat wings, and massive jaws. They are fire elementals akin to salamanders. They cannot see well, but have a good sense of smell. They are cunning and malicious, breathe fire from their mouths, and guard treasure.

    The theory that all things are composed of a combination of earth, air, fire, and water was formulated by the fifth-century

B.C.E. Greek scientist Empedocles. The idea persisted as accredited science until the seventeenth century. Following the hypothesis of the four elements and their elementals, the Neoplatonists (third century C.E.) divided these spirits into four classes, each associated with one of the elements. However, it was the sixteenth-century alchemist, doctor, and philosopher Paracelsus who gave them their familiar names. Vulcans or salamanders (from the Greek, meaning "fireplace") were designated elemental spirits of the fire. They are usually portrayed as the newts of the same name or as small dragons.

According to Paracelsus, while sylphs and undines are kindly disposed toward humans, salamanders and fire elementals can neither be approached nor approach humans themselves. He declared that while humans are made of three substances—the spiritual, the astral, and the visible or terrestrial—and exist in all three, elementals live exclusively in only one of the elements. They occupy a position between humans and pure spirits; they live in dwellings that are made of special materials "as different from the substances we know as the web of a spider is different from our linen."[1]

Some occultists believe that all fairies are elementals, spirit-beings made up of one element only—earth, air, fire, or water. The Arabian Djinn, for example, are composed of fire without smoke, with fire in their veins instead of blood. Sinistrari described creatures of an intermediate nature between the angels and humans, capable of independent thought and of choosing good or evil, composed of one of the four elements.[2] Ritual magicians, modern witches, and Pagans call upon the spirits of the four elements. They maintain that they are beings who have developed along a separate line of evolution from that of human beings.

Magically, fire rules creativity, life energy, and the spirit. Fire is the illumination within, the force of the spirit. Fire both purifies and destroys.

Divinatory Meanings: The Fire Drake appearing in a spread indicates a time of restless energy and desire for change. He may herald new opportunities, new ventures, and a cycle of great creative energy, innovation, invention, inspiration, dynamism, and passion.

Reversed Meanings: The appearance of the Fire Drake reversed in your cards indicates an unwillingness to act, vacillation, inconsistency, false starts, or projects conceived but not pursued. The card may also represent impotency, barrenness, frustration, and problems with the opposite sex.

Working with a Fire Spirit: Fire drakes or salamanders rule the element of fire. In magic, fire is concerned with passion, creativity, purification, the spirit, and energy. If you need to work on these areas of your life, you might request the aid of the fire elementals. Prepare an incense of fire by mixing a pinch of dragon's blood, two teaspoons oak chips, three teaspoons frankincense resin, half a teaspoon cinnamon powder, and a few drops of orange oil. This incense attracts fire elementals.

Say, "Ye Lords of Fire, I implore you to come to me, and to aid me in my work." Close your eyes and relax.

Imagine that it is high noon on Midsummer Day. The sun is hot and blazing. A heat-haze shimmers on the land. Forming from the haze, the fire elemental appears. Take note of his appearance and tell him your name. Ask for help with your intuitive powers and your need to change, to transform your spirit. Ask him to show you how this might be brought about. Thank the elemental, and return yourself to waking consciousness.

Two

ẄẠYLẠNẞ ṠMÍTH

The Card: The card shows a burly, elfin blacksmith working at his anvil.

The Fairy: Though most fairies are afraid of iron, some are blacksmiths. In Scandinavian myth, for example, dwarfs are supernatural smiths, dwelling deep in the earth and possessing all the secrets of magical metallurgy, forging tools for the gods, including Odin's spear and Thor's hammer. Northern European fairy smiths include Alberich and Regin, while in England there is Wayland Smith, variously described as a dwarf, elf, or giant.

Wayland Smith lives in Wayland's Smithy, a chambered, Neolithic long barrow in Berkshire, England. It is said that if a horse is tethered at the smithy under a full moon, the owner, returning in the morning, will find it newly shod. Some say that Wayland is the king of the elves.

Supernatural smiths dwell underground, beneath the mounds, or in caves, perhaps in the Land of the Dead. In stories, they sometimes possess the power to restore life, or to remake those who have wandered into their realms. There are tales of people being re-forged or rejuvenated in the smith's fire, a metaphor for shamanic initiation. Witches are traditionally called upon to forge their own athame, or black-handled knife, as part of their initiation quest, to introduce them to the mysteries of Wayland.

The Celts grouped smiths with druids as having the power of casting spells and curses: blacksmiths are the possessors of magical power. While ordinary humans hang lucky horseshoes with the points upright, so that the power does not spill out, smiths hang them point down to pour the power onto their anvils.[3]

In myth, there is a connection between trades that use fire and magic.[4] The magical reputation of the smith persisted in Europe into the nineteenth century and is still extant in India and Africa. In Britain, it was believed that smiths were blood charmers (healers) and could foretell the future. Even the water the smith used to cool metal had magical properties and was much sought after for healing purposes; a smithy-forged nail, hammered into a tree, was thought to transfer the illness to the tree.[5] Smiths also possessed the secret of the Horseman's Word, which, when whispered into the ear of the wildest horse, would calm it. People swore oaths by the smith's anvil, and in some places he had the authority to marry couples, as at the famous Gretna Green in Scotland.

In fairy stories, smiths often protect people and animals against malignant fairies, evil spirits, witchcraft, and the evil eye.

Wayland was originally a Saxon smith god (Witege, Wieland, or Voeland). In Anglo-Saxon poetry, a fine piece of smith craft was known as "the work of Wayland." Wayland made Beowulf's corselet. He is comparable to the Greek Hephaestos and the Roman Vulcan, both lame like Wayland.

Divinatory Meanings: When Wayland Smith appears in the cards, he indicates a period of hard work, creation, craftsmanship, knowledge, skill, and mastery. Opportunities and success are at hand, and your efforts will bring rewards. Wayland also indicates, in some sense, transmutation, and forging new things from the old.

Reversed Meanings: When Wayland appears reversed in your cards, he heralds rivalry, delays, and stiff competition. He may indicate inattention to detail as the cause of failure, shoddy work, and incompetence.

Working with Wayland Smith: In days gone by, every witch would have to learn the secrets of Wayland's Smith magic in order to forge their own magical tools. Today, this lesson is largely lost when magicians simply buy their tools.

Hang a horseshoe over your door to invoke the magical protection of Wayland.

THREE

GRUAGACH

The Card: A long-haired male fairy in a plaid robe is shown before a Scottish castle at the edge of a loch.

The Fairy: Gruagach means "long-haired one," and this Scottish fairy haunts castles and grand mansions, though unlike the house-dwelling brownie, it is the building it is attached to, not the family. If the house is demolished, the gruagach will disappear, never to be seen again. The spirit can be of either sex. A female gruagach once appeared on the island of Uist with long, golden hair, wore a pointed hat, and used a reed as a switch to keep her invisible cattle in order.

The gruagach manifests or cries out whenever joy or sorrow is coming to the family. At night, it tidies the castle, sweeps the floor, and rearranges the furniture. When it is heard doing so, the human inhabitants can be sure that visitors are about to arrive, and the fairy wants the place to look its best.

The gruagach is a temperamental creature; sometimes it will finish the washing, or, at other times, despite the noise of work, things may be found in disorder or a resident tradesman's tools will be ruined. If the band is not taken off the spinning wheel at night, the gruagach will muddle all the work.

When servants annoy it, the "long-haired one" will punish them by knocking over water pitchers, unmaking the beds, putting dust in the meat, or slapping people on the side of the head. As long as the fairy is honored, no bad luck will befall the family's cows. Milkmaids were always careful to appease the fairy by pouring milk on certain stones for its consumption; otherwise, the gruagach would allow the cow to trample the corn or, if further offerings were neglected, cause the death of the cow.

In Ireland, the term is more loosely applied to a variety of fairy beings, such as ogres, goblins, giants, and even human magicians, druids, and heroes.

Divinatory Meanings: The appearance of the Gruagach in your cards refers to matters concerning roots, traditions, ancestors, inheritance, family money or a family business, heirlooms, or the establishing of firm foundations in some sense.

Reversed Meanings: The Gruagach reversed indicates empty forms and rituals, going through the motions, being stuck in a rut, and boredom. There may be family disagreements about wills and legacies, or perhaps a change of residence.

Working with a Gruagach: The gruagach seems to have been more than a simple house fairy. Though the name means "long-haired one," it sometimes seems to imply a wizard or a sorcerer in some tales. They are depicted struggling with the four totem animals of the seasons—the stag (Samhain), the unicorn (Imbolc), the dragon (Beltane), and the lion (Lughnasa)—and may have appeared to turn the wheel of the seasons.[6] These fairies are said to be the spirits of ancient druids living on milk left for them by those whose priests they had once been. On the Isle of Skye, there were altars to gruagachs where offerings were left, or special "gruagach stones," perhaps a special, raised flagstone or a cairn of rocks.

You could raise your own gruagach cairn at your sacred place (or in your garden), adding a pebble to it each time you go there to meditate or perform magic. Pour offerings of milk and wine to honor the spirit each time you visit, too.

FOUR

HABETROT

The Card: The card shows a hunched, green-clad woman with a long lip, sitting by a spinning wheel. Behind her are a fairy mound and a holed standing stone.

The Fairy: Habetrot is a Lowland Scots fairy and the patroness of spinning. It is believed that a shirt woven by her is efficacious against any ill. She appears in a story that has elements of similarity with the tales of Tom Tit Tot, Rumpelstiltskin, and a host of others around the world:

Once upon a time, there was a lazy young girl who hated spinning. At every possible opportunity, she would abandon her work to go pick flowers. At last, her exasperated mother locked her up in her bedroom with her spinning wheel and five skeins of flax, saying that she wouldn't let her out until she had spun them. The girl picked up her spindle, but soon made her fingers and lips sore with her bungled attempts. Bursting into tears, she climbed through the bedroom window and fled into the fields.

Wandering disconsolately near the stream, she found a self-holed stone, through which—as everyone knows—one can see fairies. Peering through the cleft, the girl was amazed to see into a fairy mound where a strange little woman sat spinning, pulling out the thread with a huge, long lip.

"Why have you got such a long lip?" asked the girl, somewhat impolitely.

"From pulling out the thread, lassie," replied the old woman, who was none other than the fairy Habetrot. The girl was soon chatting away to the old fairy, complaining that she couldn't spin and explaining the task her mother had given her. Habetrot told the wee lassie to bring the five skeins of flax to her, and the fairies would do the job. No sooner said than done, the yarn was fetched and the fairies, all with long lips and hunched backs from sitting so long over their spinning wheels, spun the thread.

"Tis finished, Scantlie Mab!" cried Habetrot to one of the other fairies, "though the wee lassie little knows that my name is Habetrot!" She returned the thread to the girl, and advised her not to tell her mother who really had spun the thread.

The mother was delighted with the smooth thread, and ran back and forth boasting how her daughter had spun so well. A passing laird thought what a good wife the girl would make, and married her, bragging of all the spinning she would do after the wedding. He presented his bride with a new spinning wheel and plenty of fresh flax.

The unhappy girl went down to the holed stone and called on Habetrot. The kindly fairy considered the problem and advised the girl to bring her husband to visit the fairy spinners. The couple was shown into the mound, and the laird was horrified at the deformed backs and lips of the women.

"Yes, we were all bonnie once, until we took up the spinning," Habetrot said. "Yon girl will soon be the same after pulling out the thread with her sweet, red lips and bending her lovely, young back over the wheel!"

"She will not!" exclaimed the laird, horrified at the prospect of his lovely, young bride losing her looks. He took his wife home and forbade her to do any spinning, passing it all on to the fairies instead. So all worked out well in the end.

Divinatory Meanings: When Habetrot appears in your cards, she indicates the workings of fate and destiny. Habetrot spins you a change of fortune. You will make progress; there will be advancement, accomplishment, new opportunities, and perhaps a change of career.

Reversed Meanings: The reversed card indicates a run of bad luck. You may be surprised and disconcerted by the turn of events, but these are fated and cannot be avoided.

Working with Habetrot: Habetrot is an aspect of the ancient goddess who spins the thread of life. Her spindle whorl is the revolving planets, her wheel the spirals of the Milky Way, and her thread is life itself. She orders the universe and the destiny of each person. The following pathworking is an encounter with this goddess:

Relax. Imagine that you are walking on a hillside on a warm summer evening. You see golden lights shining from a marble temple on the top of the hill, and you decide to investigate.

As you arrive at the temple, the door stands open and you enter. Inside is an old woman, bent over a weaving loom. Behind her is a spinning wheel. She beckons you to look at what she is doing.

You realize the picture she is weaving is the story of your life—you can see your past and present and threads leading toward the future. You study it for a while. Can you see what forces are shaping the pattern of your life?

After a time, you feel her gentle hand on your arm and see that she is smiling at you. She leads you outside and gestures for you to look around you.

As you look, you see that shining threads connect the herbs and the trees, and the rocks and the birds that fly in the night sky. Shining threads connect the earth and the stars.

She touches your solar plexus, and you can see that from a glowing point in the center of your body, shining threads emerge, which connect you to the earth, the trees, and even the planets moving in the heavens. Through the threads you become aware of the thoughts of the scurrying animals, the lofty existence of the trees, and the life of the earth. You become aware of how all things are connected and dependent on each other. Spend some time enjoying this experience.

When you are ready to return, thank the lady, and allow the scene to fade around you. Allow yourself to return to waking consciousness.

FIVE

CRO SÍTH/TAROO USHTY

The Card: The card shows a white cow with red ears beside a lake in which is reflected a taroo ushty, or water bull.

The Fairies: Fairies are very interested in cattle. They keep herds of cattle themselves, customarily under a lake or beneath the sea where the animals graze on seaweed. Occasionally one of these *cro sith*, or "fairy cows," appears on the shore as a gift for a human farmer. He is fortunate, as it will provide an endless supply of milk.

There are several legends of fairy cattle left as gifts, identified by their round ears. In stories, they are often called "dun cows," a dun being a fairy mound. There are many dun cows in Scottish and English fairy lore, such as the Dun Cow of McBrandy's Thicket and the Dun Cow of Kirkham.

From Wales, too, come legends of fairy cows, including one called Fuwch Gyfeiliorn. This cow belonged to a band of fairies from the region of Llyn Barfog, a lake near Aberdovey in Wales. At dusk the fairies appear, clad all in green, accompanied by their milk-white hounds and milk-white cattle. Once, a farmer caught one of these cows and his fortune was made: it produced such butter, milk, and cheese as had never been seen. He called the cow Fuwch Gyfeiliorn, and its fame spread. The farmer became rich beyond his wildest dreams, until one day he stupidly got it into his head that the fairy cow was getting old and he ought to fatten her for slaughter. The fatal day arrived and despite the pleading eyes of the cow, the butcher raised his arm and struck her a dreadful blow. Suddenly there was an almighty shriek, and the bludgeon went right through the head of the cow and felled nine men standing nearby. To everyone's astonishment, a green lady arose from the lake and softly called to the cow. Together they disappeared back beneath the waters, never to be seen again.[7]

Otherworldly cattle are common in British and Irish lore, recognized by their red or round ears. A herd of cattle descended from fairy cows have grazed the parkland around Chillingham Castle in Northumberland (northern England) since the thirteenth century. They have the red ears and white coats of fairy cattle, and it is said that they will kill anyone who touches them.

• • •

It follows that if there are fairy cows, there must be fairy bulls. Bulls were sacred animals to the Celts, representing energy, fertility, virility, potency, and vigor. Any bulls that died naturally were buried as an offering to the gods of the earth, while two snow-white bulls were sacrificed to the sky gods at the time of the gathering of the sacred mistletoe.

Fairy water bulls live in lochs and rivers, coming ashore to lead ordinary cattle beneath the waters to Fairyland. For this reason, farmers will not graze cattle near water.

The taroo ushty is a fearsome water bull that lives in the seas surrounding the Isle of Man. It sometimes leaves the sea to feed and mate with domestic cows, and the resulting offspring will be fat and sleek, producing copious amounts of milk. However, the taroo ushty has a fierce temperament, hates humans, and has been know to terrorize whole neighborhoods. One farmer had to abandon his farm when the taroo ushty turned against him.

Divinatory Meanings (Cro Sith): When the gentle and protective Cro Sith appears upright in your cards, she heralds a situation of nurturing and unselfish love of the kind a mother has for her child. Her gifts are comfort, support, shelter, caring, and emotional nourishment.

Reversed Meanings (Taroo Ushty): When the fierce Taroo Ushty appears in your cards, he indicates aggressiveness and power misused, brute force, and arrogance.

Working with the Fairy Cow: This pathworking explores the nurturing aspects of the fairy cow:

Relax. It is a warm, balmy evening in the summer. You find yourself in a meadow under the open sky. Around you the grass is lush and sweetly scented and you catch the perfume of night flowers.

Red and white cows patiently chew the grass, moving slowly and deliberately with a stateliness all their own. One suckles her calf, and you can see the droplets of snow-white milk on its muzzle. Everything is very peaceful and calm.

You lie down on the grass and feel the earth support you comfortably. The earth sustains you, supports you. You feel its power. The earth nurtures you. The earth heals you. Feel its power flow into you.

You stare up at the stars, the Milky Way, the galaxy where our little planet is situated, which the ancients believed was milk from the breasts of the Mother Goddess who often takes the form of a cow. You feel the light of the stars on your skin as a physical touch. It enters your body and nourishes your spirit. You are a child of the universe.

When you are ready to leave, thank the spirit of the Mother. Let the scene fade around you, and return to waking consciousness.

Working with the Taroo Ushty: While the fairy cow is the nurturing mother, the taroo ushty stands for the ruthless destruction of those who despoil the natural world. His energies are dangerous to invoke.

Six

AINE

The Card: A lovely female fairy sits beside a fairy mound, on a bright summer day.

The Fairy: The fairy Aine was sitting one day by Lough Gur (Ireland) when the Earl of Desmond chanced to see her combing her hair and instantly fell in love with her. In one version of the tale, he made her his wife by seizing her clothes so she couldn't escape; in another, she agreed to marry him on the condition that he would never be surprised by anything that their children did. Unfortunately, when their son, the Earl of Fitzgerald, jumped in and out of a bottle, he couldn't help but be amazed. Poor Fitzgerald turned into a wild goose and flew away, while Aine fled into the mound still known as Cnoc Aine in County Limerick.

Originally a deity of the Irish gods Tuatha dé Danaan, Aine was once the patroness of sovereignty, the goddess of human love, crops, horses, and cattle. Like many of the old gods, she was demoted to the status of a fairy. Her older legends are less pretty and relate how she revenged her rape by Aillil Olom, the king of Munster, by slaying him with magic. Her feast day is Midsummer Eve, when she appears at Cnoc Aine, surrounded by maidens. Local people once gathered there to hold torchlight processions through the fields of ripening crops. The first Friday, Saturday, and Sunday after Lughnasa (August 1) are also sacred to her. It was said that she would claim a human life on those days.

Aine is served by the Dinnshenchas, shapeshifting Irish fairies that protect cattle and avenge women harmed or raped by men.

The meadowsweet flower is sacred to Aine, and she gave the plant its scent. In one legend, she was pursued by St. Patrick, who was intent on purging Ireland of its Pagan gods; but she spread the flower behind her so that its scent confused the chase and St. Patrick failed to exorcise her.

Divinatory Meanings: When the fairy Aine appears upright in your cards, she heralds harmony, new romance, marriage, commitment, friendship, partnerships, and cooperation.

Reversed Meanings: When Aine appears reversed in the cards, she suggests unreal expectations for a relationship, resentments, inequality, bias, injustice, quarrels, misunderstandings, separation, divorce, love not returned, inequitable regard, or unfaithfulness.

Working with Aine: Aine means "brightness," "heat," or "speed," and the word is cognate to the Latin *ignis*, meaning "fire."

Aine's festival is Midsummer, marked by a torchlight procession about her hill led by young women and a vigil held
around a bonfire until dawn. The festival celebrates the height
of the sun's power. Farmers carried torches of straw around
Cnoc Aine, then dispersed themselves among their fields and
pastures, waving the flames over their cattle and crops—a way
of carrying the sun's blessing of prosperity through fire. On
Midsummer Eve, light a candle in the name of Aine and carry
it around your property to solicit her blessing.

Meadowsweet is the sacred flower of Aine and can be used
to contact her. The dried flowers can be used in incense, and
the fresh flowers in garlands, bouquets, and decorations. Anoint
your forehead and forearms with meadowsweet oil while in-
voking Aine at Midsummer.

Aine's Meadowsweet Oil: Loosely fill a jar with meadowsweet
flowers and add enough vegetable oil to cover them. Leave in
a warm place and shake daily for two weeks. Strain and bottle.

SEVEN

WILL O' THE WISP

The Card: The image shows a little fairy with a lantern, flitting over marshy ground.

The Fairy: Will o' the wisps are bog fairies who appear as curious lights, usually seen flickering in the distance over swamps and marshes. They jump and dance along with the aim of leading travelers astray.

    The will o' the wisp has many local names, such as Billy wi' t' Wisp, Jenny Burnt Tale, Peggy wi' the Lanthern, Elf Light, Fox Fire, Hinky Punk, and so on. Perhaps the most common name is Jack-a-lantern, or Jack-o'-lantern. Until the fenland swamps of East Anglia were drained at the beginning of the twentieth century, Jack-o'-lanterns commonly haunted the marshes at night. Their glowing flames bewitched travelers and led them to their deaths in deep bogs. Shakespeare used the expression "played the Jack with us" in *The Tempest*. Whistling is said to attract them, and to escape their clutches, you should lie facedown on the path until they go away. The name jack-o'-lantern is now given to the hollowed-out pumpkins or turnips that are used as lanterns at Halloween.

In Wales, the will o' the wisp is called *ellylldan*, meaning "fire fairy." It can be seen dancing about on marshy ground, into which it may lead a hapless traveler. Iolo the Bard described an encounter with an ellylldan during which he followed it down from a mountaintop into a boggy valley. It waited for him every time he stopped, but each time dwindled away almost to a spark until he began moving again, when it would glow and glide on.[8]

The will o' the wisp of Guernsey lore is the *faëu boulanger*, meaning "the rolling fire." It manifests as a ball of fire, and a number of people have been astonished to find it rolling straight toward them. It is thought to be a spirit in pain, cursed to wander and vainly attempt to free itself from its suffering by suicide. It guards a hidden treasure.

When the will o' the wisp appears at sea, it is generally called St. Elmo's fire. It is accompanied by a crackling sound and is seen on ships' masts. When sailors see it, they know that the worst of the storm is over. St. Elmo is a corruption of St. Erasmus, who died during a storm at sea in the fourth century C.E. He told the sailors that he would come back from the dead and show himself to them if they were destined to be saved from the tempest. Sure enough, the light appeared at the masthead.

Some say that will o' the wisp lights are the souls of dead children or the ghosts of greedy men with hidden treasure, or people neither good enough for heaven nor evil enough for hell.

Divinatory Meanings: The appearance of the Will o' the Wisp betokens illusion, fallacy, or a false impression. He may indicate self-delusion and wishful thinking over some matter.

Reversed Meanings: The Will o' the Wisp reversed indicates faithless friends, false or broken promises, and unreliability.

Working with the Will o' the Wisp: Not recommended.

EÍGHT

TAM LÍN

The Card: The card shows a handsome knight, standing beside a
well, deep in the forest. Wild roses grow over the water, and
the knight holds several lovely blossoms in his hand.

The Fairy: There once was a golden-haired girl called Janet who
dressed in fairy green. She was the fairest maiden for many a
mile and so bold as to be the despair of her father. One day
she went into Carterhaugh Wood (in the Scottish Border
country) to pick wild roses. No sooner had she plucked a single blossom than a tall, handsome elf appeared before her. The
pair dallied together all that afternoon and fell in love. When
Janet left, she was no longer a maiden, but carried the fairy's
child.

It was not long before her father's household guessed that she was pregnant, and pressed her to name the father. They laughed when she told them it was a handsome elf, and she blushed with shame. Eventually she was driven to return to the woods and find the fairy man once more. On All Hallows Eve, she crept shivering through the dark woods and called for her fairy lover. The elf appeared. He told her that he was really not a fairy at all, but a human knight under enchantment, held in bondage to the Fairy Queen. His name was Tam Lin, and he was the grandson of the Earl of Roxburgh. He had been hunting one day and had fallen from his horse, only to be caught by the Fairy Queen. The woods belonged to her, and he guarded it by day and went forth with the Fairy Rade by night. Janet was determined to rescue him, an endeavor that her lover explained was possible, but full of danger.

As instructed, the next evening on Hallowday, Janet proceeded to the crossroads and hid behind a thorn bush to await the passing of the Fairy Rade. Eventually, to the sweet sound of the music of lutes and pipes, a procession came into view, led by the lovely Fairy Queen riding a black horse, and followed by pale fairy lords and ladies. Among them was Tam Lin on a milk-white horse, recognizable by the fact that he was wearing only one glove. Janet sprang out from her hiding place and pulled him from his saddle.

By malignant fairy glamour, Tam Lin was transformed into an adder, and Janet nearly lost her grip. Then the coiling snake became a lion. Janet was terrified, but hung on. The lion became a red-hot iron bar. Janet knew it would not hurt her: this was the father of her child. It was the last transformation, and she cast the bar into the well. There it steamed for an instant, and a moment later a naked man stepped from the well; her lover Tam Lin had become human again.

The Fairy Queen blazed with anger. She turned her gaze on Tam Lin, amazed that a mortal could have bested her. She cried that had she known that a woman could have won him, she would have torn his heart from him and given him one of stone. At this, she wheeled away, all her band following, and disappeared into the trees.

Divinatory Meanings: The appearance of Tam Lin indicates restoration, release from a bad or frightening situation, recovery from illness, relief, pleasure after pain, or a weight lifted from the mind.

Reversed Meanings: The reversed card indicates restriction, imprisonment of some kind, banishment, loss, guilt, and fear, or perhaps bad health.

Working with Tam Lin: Though Tam Lin and Janet were not fairies, but victims of the Fairy Queen, their lesson is an important one. Their love, and Janet's bravery and determination, freed them from a frightening situation that seemed impossible to resolve.

JENNY GREENTEETH

NINE

JENNY GREENTEETH

The Card: The card shows a hag fairy rising from a river. Her hair is composed of waterweeds and her teeth are also green.

The Fairy: Jenny Greenteeth is a water fairy of the River Ribble in northern England. When green weeds wave in the flowing water, it indicates that Jenny is lurking beneath the surface, ready to take another victim. She haunts the steppingstones near Brungerley and every seven years claims a human life by grabbing some hapless traveler and pulling him beneath the water to drown. Children are warned not to go near the water, or Jenny Greenteeth will take them.

Jenny is only one such fairy. Peg Prowler haunts the River Tees. She also has green hair and sharp teeth. If people enter the water, she grabs their ankles and drags them beneath the surface. Another fairy called Peg O'Nell also demands the sacrifice of a life every seven years and will be satisfied with a small animal or bird, though if this is not offered, she will take a human life.

The River Ribble was sacred to Minerva during the Roman occupation of Britain and to an unknown water goddess before that, and Jenny is likely to be a folk memory of this goddess. Human sacrifices may once have been made to the water deities, which may account for predatory figures such as Jenny.

Such lore survives in folktales, like the story of the Scottish guardian water-demons. It is said that in older times, when a castle was sacked, a crafty servant might contrive to throw some portion of the family treasure into a nearby pool. On one occasion, a diver was brought in to bring the treasure to the surface, but when he dived, he encountered the water guardian of the lake, who told him to leave immediately and not come back. However, the diver disobeyed, and moments after his second dive, his heart and lungs were found floating on the surface of the water, torn out by the demon.[9]

Water has often been considered to be a living thing, or certainly to have the power of sustaining, bestowing, and even restoring life—as well as being capable of taking it. Every ancient society honored springs, wells, and water sources as sacred. The Celts and other tribes sacrificed treasure to lake and river spirits. At the site of Flag Fen in Cambridgeshire (England), over three hundred bronze artifacts were found, including pins and ornaments, rings, and a large number of weapons, including swords and daggers and tools such a chisels and awls.[10]

Divinatory Meanings: When Jenny Greenteeth surfaces in your cards, she indicates danger and uncertainty—some pitfall or hazard lies in your path. Something that appears secure has a deceptive appearance; a wolf in sheep's clothing may fool you.

Reversed Meanings: When Jenny Greenteeth appears reversed in your cards, she indicates a necessary sacrifice, albeit an unwilling one. You will have to give up one thing in order to gain another.

Working with Jenny Greenteeth: Not recommended.

LADY

THE GREEN LADY

THE LADY OF THE SUMMER COURT
THE GREEN LADY

The Card: The card shows an auburn-haired forest fairy, clad in mossy green.

The Fairy: In England, *green lady* is a term for dryads, or tree spirits, dwelling in oak, elm, apple, willow, holly, and yew trees. Permission had to be sought from the fairy before chopping down any tree, and primroses were planted beneath the trees as an offering to the Green Lady to solicit her blessings. Green, of course, is the color of growing things, and many nature fairies wear green dresses, jackets, or caps. Some even have green skin. In Scotland and Ireland, green is exclusively a fairy color, and until recently was considered very unlucky for humans to wear—my grandmother absolutely forbade the wearing of green clothes.

Many people instinctively feel that a tree has a spirit or consciousness. In the early days of Buddhism, this was a matter of some controversy, and it was decided that trees did not have souls like humans, but had certain resident spirits, called *dewas*, who spoke from within them. Occultists use the term *devas* to describe the resident spirit of a tree or other plant.

Tree spirits have been honored since ancient times. Since trees can live for many centuries, some for thousands of years, they witness far more than we humans can in our short lives. Our ancestors therefore believed that tree spirits must be very wise. The spirits of evergreen trees were particularly powerful, since they can withstand the force of winter, when other trees shed their leaves and become dormant. Trees were honored at festivals with wreaths and decorations. From this connection of the tree deity with virility comes the custom of carrying tree sprigs in a wedding bouquet, as well as May Day observances such as the leaf-clad Jack in the Green dancer, which celebrates the return of vegetation in the summer. We still honor the spirit of the tree when we decorate the evergreen Christmas tree and place the fairy, which represents its living spirit, at the top.

Divinatory Meanings: When the gentle Green Lady appears in your cards, she indicates growth, progress, moving forward, expansion, vitality, energy, virility, and potency.

The Green Lady may also represent a real person in the life of the questioner: an attractive woman who is clever, hard working, loyal, resourceful, passionate, enthusiastic, and quick to respond emotionally, either with love or anger.

Reversed Meanings: The Green Lady reversed indicates a lack of energy, ennui, loss of vitality, fatigue, and a lack of real purpose or direction. She may also reveal feelings of envy and jealousy.

The Green Lady reversed may be a real person in your life: a lazy woman who is easily bored or discouraged, but who demands attention and comfort for her largely imagined ills.

Working with the Green Lady: The Green Lady is the protector of the forest and all growing things. She will be angry if you bend the saplings and strip the bark from her trees. If you wish to take wood or herbs from the forest, you must seek her sanction. Mark the plant you want with a piece of thread, then tell the Green Lady why you want its gifts, asking her permission to take it. If you don't think you've received a reply, or are not sure, leave it alone. Only take a little of any one plant, and don't strip it bare so that the plant will die, or the Green Lady will not welcome you back into her domain. Traditionally, you should leave her an offering of three handfuls of flax seed.

THE KNAVE OF THE SUMMER COURT
ROBIN GOODFELLOW

The Card: The card shows a woodland fairy with horns and hooves, playing a pipe.

The Fairy: Robin Goodfellow is a mischievous English fairy. As Shakespeare wrote in *A Midsummer Night's Dream:*

> *. . . that shrude and knavish sprite*
> *Call'd Robin Goodfellow; are you not he*
> *That frights the maidens of the villagery;*
> *Skim milk, and sometimes labour in the quern*
> *And bootless make the breathless housewife churn;*
> *And sometime make the drink to bear no barm;*

Mislead night wanderers, laughing at their harm?
Those that Hobgoblin call you, and sweet Puck,
You do their work, and they should have good luck.

This shows that while he often played practical jokes on people, by appearing as a pony, a hare, or a will o' the wisp, sometimes he could be as helpful as a brownie. It may seem strange to many people today, but the ordinary folks of England believed absolutely in the spirits of the greenwood. Robin Goodfellow was one of the most widely known, though Reginald Scot wrote in 1584 that belief in him wasn't as widespread as it had been. Nevertheless, he remained a popular figure in ballads and mummers' plays for many years after this date.

Robin Goodfellow has the head of a handsome boy and the feet of a goat, small horns on his head, and carries musical pipes with which he bewitches humans. It may be that he is the fairy remnant of some ancient horned god. He is never seen between Halloween and the vernal equinox and is usually accompanied by a variety of animals. He may be synonymous with the horned god Cernunnos, or with Robin Hood as a spirit or god of the forest. He has a lusty nature and likes to seduce human girls. The Puritans called him a devil and condemned him along with all the other fairies.

Some later tales make Robin Goodfellow synonymous with Puck, including Shakespeare's *A Midsummer Night's Dream,* though he is generally more benevolent. Puck is sometimes described as the jester of the fairy court and appears in this role in *A Midsummer Night's Dream.* In parts of Worcestershire, peasants claimed to be "Poake led" into ditches and bogs by the mysterious fairy before it disappeared with a loud laugh. In the Midlands, this was called being "pouk-ledden."

Puck is related to the Welsh *pwca* and the Irish *phooka,* the Norwegian *pukje,* the Danish *puge,* the Swedish *puke,* the old Norse *puki,* the Latvian *pukis,* the German *puks,* and the Baltic *puk.*

Divinatory Meanings: When Robin Goodfellow bounds into your cards, he heralds fun and good-hearted mischief. There are adventures in the offing, new experiences, entertainment, and celebrations.

Robin Goodfellow may indicate a real person in your life: a young man who is fearless, witty, impetuous, and unpredictable, and who is always ready for excitement. He is quick-tempered, but hates injustice of any kind, and will speak out against it.

Reversed Meanings: Robin Goodfellow reversed indicates delays, postponements, minor irritations, and perhaps legal problems.

Robin Goodfellow reversed may indicate a real person in your life: a young man who is narrow-minded, bigoted, argumentative, and a lover of opposition for its own sake.

Working with Robin Goodfellow: Robin Goodfellow is the blithe spirit of the greenwood. The following pathworking explores this:

Relax. Imagine that you are deep within the greenwood one warm summer afternoon. You are following a path through the undergrowth, flanked with starry woodland flowers. It winds around the ancient trees and bushes hung with sweet-smelling wild honeysuckle.

You can hear the mellifluous piping of a flute, borne on the air. It gets louder as you follow the path into a clearing. There in its center is Robin Goodfellow, a merry-faced elf with little horns on his forehead, and the furry legs and hooves of a goat. He sits amid a gathering of forest animals, deer and stags, foxes, hares, rabbits, badgers, hedgehogs, and birds. They are quiet and peaceful in his presence, their ancient enmities forgotten under his influence.

You gaze in wonder and are filled with joy that such a thing is possible. If you wish, you can speak to Robin and ask him to tell you some of the secrets of the wildwood. You might learn from the animals that sit at his feet, for each has its own lesson to teach. Stay as long as you like.

When you are ready to return, allow the scene to fade around you, and return yourself to waking consciousness.

THE QUEEN OF THE SUMMER COURT

THE ELDER QUEEN

The Card: The card shows a mature female fairy, amid a grove of flowering elder trees. She is dressed in woodland colors of yellow and green and holds out a plate of elderberries. There is a radiance about her head. Elder flowers can be seen at the bottom corner of the card.

The Fairy: A spirit inhabits the elder, and for this reason, if it is cut at Midsummer—when it flowers—it is reputed to bleed real blood. In England, the guardian fairy is called the Elder Mother or Elder Queen. She lives at its roots and is the mother of the elves. If you stand under an elder on Midsummer Eve, you will see the King of the Elves pass by.

In Lincolnshire, it was believed that cutting elder wood without the permission of the Old Girl offended her, and she took revenge on anyone who felled her tree by striking down his livestock with disease. Permission must be sought as follows: "Owd Gal, give me some of thy wood and Oi will give thee some of moine, when I graws inter a tree." Farmers took the revenge of the Elder Queen so seriously that when a new field was cleared, the elder trees were generally left standing and had to be plowed around. Gypsies will never cut down an elder or burn elder wood.

One Derbyshire legend tells of a farmer who, every Midsummer Eve, climbed a hill behind his cottage to lay primroses at the foot of the three elders that grew at its summit. On his deathbed, he instructed his three sons to carry on the tradition. The two eldest lads scorned this, and only the younger continued the custom. This "superstition" annoyed the other brothers, and one of them went up the hill and chopped down one of the trees. He was instantly struck down by an illness. For days he withered on his bed and finally died. The second brother felled another of the trees and his end was the same. Only the youngest brother and one tree remained. All his life, primroses graced the fairy tree each year on Midsummer Eve.

It is safe to take a branch from the elder on January 6 without permission if you spit on the ground three times. This elder branch can then be used to draw a magic circle in a lonely place for the purpose of demanding magic fern seed, which will give you the strength of thirty men. The Elder Queen will see that an unseen hand delivers a chalice containing the seed.

The elder tree is associated with witches, who are often said to gain their knowledge from fairies. Sometimes the elder tree is a witch herself or has a witch living in it. The elder was a Celtic sacred tree, associated with the crone goddess, and it is often treated with great caution and surrounded with warnings as a result. In Ireland, witches used elder sticks for their broom staffs, not ash.

Elder has a reputation as a tree of protection, and a charm to safeguard livestock was made by tying two pieces together with red twine. It is said that if you stand beneath an elder, you will never be struck by lightning, and that a cottage may be similarly protected by planting an elder next to it.

Divinatory Meanings: When the Elder Mother appears in your cards, she indicates grace, warmth, protection, kindness, strength, and help from a friend. She may also denote the success of a venture.

The card may indicate a real person in your life: a mature woman who is forthright, open, honest, practical, energetic, helpful, and generous. She will probably have a welcoming, well-kept home.

Reversed Meanings: When the Elder Queen appears reversed in your cards, she warns you to be conscientious in your work, or you will make a bad mistake with unpleasant consequences. Tread carefully in all that you do, at the present time. A project may have been initiated, but there are still possible pitfalls ahead.

The reversed card may represent a real woman in your life: a woman who is mature and self-sufficient, with an inner strength and determination.

Working with the Elder Mother: Where the elder grows, the Goddess is not far away. To connect with the Elder Mother, you can use the bounty of the elder tree. Flutes made of elder wood are used to summon the fairies. It is a tree connected with witches, and the handle of the coven sword is traditionally made from elder wood.

The sweet blossom can be collected in June at the full moon. A single head of flowers infused in a cup of boiling water will make a tisane that can be drunk to make contact with the Elder Mother. The flowers can be dried and added to incense, where they act as a fixative. They attract dryads and fairies when the incense is burned.

Elder leaves should be gathered on Midsummer morning for magical purposes and extra healing power. For a soothing ointment, stew a handful for thirty minutes in two ounces of petroleum jelly, strain, and pour into a jar.

The berries should be collected in early autumn. They can be made into teas, wines, jams, and jellies, or used as an herbal dye.

During the winter, the Elder Mother becomes the Crone. If you can find any berries in December, these are a rare and potent gift of the Goddess, and any wine made from them will be a mighty sabbat brew. Use sparingly as an aid to clairvoyance.

The King of the Summer Court

The Oakman

The Card: The card shows an oak wood in early summer; there are bluebells on the ground. Before the tree is a dwarfish male fairy holding an acorn cup. He is accompanied by a fox.

The Fairy: Oakmen are the most widespread tree fairies in England; sometimes they are merged with oak trees, and sometimes they appear as forest dwarfs who offer tempting food to passing mortals, which will turn out to be poisonous fungi disguised by fairy glamour. They inhabit copses where saplings have grown from felled oaks. If bluebells are growing in a copse, it invariably indicates the presence of oakmen, and mortals should be warned to avoid the area.

Oakmen become extremely angry and dangerous if their tree is cut down. It was said that when an oak is felled, it gives out shrieks and groans that can be heard a mile away.

Oakmen also guard all the forest animals and punish those who harm them, such as foxhunters. However, they also possess beneficial magic; the rain that gathers in their oak hollows has powerful, magical healing qualities.

The oak tree (*Quercus robur*) has manifold associations with fairies. The majority of fairies are found in woods and forests, particularly oak groves. Elves and fairies are often said to dwell within the hollow trunks of oaks. A New Forest rhyme advises to "turn your cloaks for fairy folks are in old oaks" (turning your cloak inside out protects you from being distracted from your path by fairies). The concept of tree spirits is ancient and very widespread. In Greek myth, dryads and hamadryads are the spirits of the trees themselves.

The oak is a tree that is perhaps more honored in lore than any other. The Roman writer Pliny recognized that the Greek *drus*, meaning "oak" or "oak spirit," is related to the Celtic word *druid*. Some authors suggest that the second syllable may be related to the Indo-European *wid*, meaning "know," and the derived meaning would be "oak knowledge." It has been proposed that *bard* may be formed from the word *barr*, meaning "branch," as *bard* in Welsh is *bardd*. The Celts carved god statues from oak boughs, which were kept in the sacred grove of oaks. On the island of Anglesey there are still traces of the ancient oak groves of the druids. An oak coppice or grove near Loch Siant on the Isle of Skye was so sacred that no one would enter it, even into the nineteenth century.

Oaks were often designated local meeting places, a practice that goes back to druidic times but persisted well into the recent past, with Gospel Oaks being popular locations for itinerant Christian preachers.

Divinatory Meanings: When the mighty Oakman appears in your spread, he indicates power, good government, received knowledge, and authority. His gifts are willpower and self-control, and the Oakman promises that if you act correctly and honorably, you will be rewarded.

The Oakman may represent a real person in your life: a mature man in a position of authority. He is reliable, honest, practical, methodical, and conscientious. He loves his family and traditions.

Reversed Meanings: The Oakman reversed indicates idleness, complacency, inertia, a fear of change, and the inability to adapt to changing circumstances. He points to the failure to seize opportunities or to follow up on promising openings.

The Oakman reversed may personify a real person in your life: a mature man who is materialistic, uncaring about anything except his own interests, ruthless, and unable to see anyone else's point of view.

Working with the Oakman: Trees are honored for the knowledge they gain during their long lives. Witches sometimes simply meditate with their backs to trees to communicate with their energies. Sometimes a tree will allow you to take a branch of living wood that connects with its knowledge and power, no matter how far from the tree it is taken. This is called a wand, and to be given one by the tree spirit is a great honor that must be earned, and never stolen.

For a real magic wand, the wood should be taken from the living tree to capture its essence. This is the subject of much misunderstanding. Some say that the wood must be taken in such a way as to capture the dryad of the tree, but this is a kind of shorthand for something much more profound. Every plant has its own spirit, which embodies its character, its magical vibration, its lessons, and its complex connection within the

Web of Being. Plants and trees must be approached as individuals, and respected as living, spiritual entities. No two oak trees have the same personality, and no two flax plants have the same qualities. To capture this spirit is a difficult business; it is not simply a matter of walking around a tree three times and saying, "Can I have a branch?" then lopping one off, and leaving a coin in return (what the tree is supposed to do with this is anybody's guess). How many people know when they do have an answer? Is the plant even listening? Such instructions are based on folklore, a shadow of the true knowledge.

First, a relationship must be established with a tree spirit over a period of time; you must understand each other. Some trees are well-disposed toward humankind, some need to be persuaded, some fought, and some will never give you anything no matter what you do. Steal their wood, and you will simply have a dead twig, not a living wand.

When you have your wand, which traditionally measures from elbow to fingertip, it may be carved with your personal symbols, but should not have any crystals incorporated into it.

1. Paracelsus (1493–1541), in his *Treatise on Elemental Sprites*.

2. Louis Marie Sinistrari (1622–1701), *Daemonalitas*.

3. Janet and Stewart Farrar, *The Witches' God* (London: Hale, 1989).

4. Mircea Eliade, *The Forge and the Crucible* (Rider, 1962).

5. There is a park, opposite the forge in my village, where nails are still hammered into trees for this purpose.

6. Kaledon Naddair, *Keltic Folk and Fairy Tales* (London: Century, 1987).

7. Wirt Sikes, *British Goblins: The Realm of the Faerie* (1880; reprint, Llanerch facsimile edition, 1991).

8. Ibid.

9. Walter Gregor, *Notes on the Folk-Lore of North-East Scotland* (London: 1881).

10. Marion K. Pearce, "Flag Fen Lake Village," *Silver Wheel* (February 1997).

The
Autumn
Court

ꓮCE

ꓮCE

MERMAID

The Image: The card shows a mermaid: the upper half of her body is that of an attractive woman, and the lower half is like a fish tail, covered in scales. Her hair is long and glossy. She sits on a rock, which emerges from the sea at twilight. The evening star Venus can be seen in the sky. Her mirror lies in the corner of the card, reflecting the face of the full moon.

The Fairy: Mermaids are sea fairies with the upper bodies of lovely women and the tails of fish, though in early Celtic tales they were simply sea-dwelling maidens. Sometimes these exotic creatures come to the surface of the sea and sit on rocks near the shore, combing their beautiful hair. The mermaid is an en-

chantress, a seductive siren with a sweet voice, but her songs
lure ships onto the rocky coasts of Scotland and Cornwall.
They take the souls of drowned sailors to the bottom of the
sea, where they keep them in lobster pots. Anyone who falls
asleep on the beach is in danger of being taken by the mermaid to live with her in her underwater palace.

The earliest stories of mermaids date from around 5000
B.C.E., and sailors have been reporting sightings ever since.
Alexander the Great captured two mermaids with skin as white
as snow and hair that came down to their feet. Another mermaid was washed ashore in fifteenth-century Holland and became a maidservant. Belief in mermaids was still widespread in
coastal areas of Britain in the nineteenth century, and as recently
as 1947 an eighty-year-old fisherman from the Isle of Muck
claimed he had seen a mermaid near the shore, combing her
hair.

There are many tales of marriages between mermaids and
human men. Mermaids make good wives and caring mothers.
However, they are usually unwilling to leave their watery home,
and men in love with mermaids have to resort to subterfuge. If
her magical cap, belt, or comb is hidden, she is unable to leave
the land, but as soon as she finds it, she will return to the sea,
leaving her husband and children without a second thought.

Mermaids may derive from such ancient goddesses as
Aphrodite, who was born from the foam of the sea and rode
to the shore in a seashell. In early astrology, her mirror was the
emblem that represented the planet Venus.

Divinatory Meanings: The Mermaid is most at home in the
water, the element that symbolizes emotions and feelings.
When she appears upright in your spread, she heralds a time
of great fulfillment and joy. This may be a time of creative inspiration when you create works of great truth and beauty.
The Mermaid may also be a harbinger of love, attraction, pas-

sion, and marriage. She emphasizes the importance of female sensuality.

Reversed Meanings: While water can be cleansing and free-flowing, it can also be dammed up and fetid. The Mermaid reversed in your cards indicates a time of emotional stagnation and loneliness, unhappiness, isolation, barrenness, and despair.

Working with a Water Elemental: The mermaid is an elemental creature of water. In magic, water rules emotions, intuition, clairvoyant powers, instinct, and the subconscious.

Prepare an incense of water by mixing half a teaspoon daisy petals, a few drops of jasmine oil, three teaspoons myrrh resin, two teaspoons willow wood, and one teaspoon white rose petals. Burn on a charcoal block. This incense attracts water elementals.

Say, "Ye creature of water, I implore you to come to me, and to aid me in my work."

Close your eyes and relax. Imagine it is twilight on an autumn evening. You stand before a deep pool, and as you gaze into it, the water elemental rises from it. Take note of its appearance and tell it your name. Ask for help with your emotions and your ability to love others and yourself. Imagine swimming freely in the warm ocean, supported, gently moving with the ebb and flow of the waves. Though the current affects you, altering your course, you don't care; you glory in its patterns and changes. Be aware of the ebb and flow of life, sometimes calm, sometimes stormy. You see the patterns at work in your own life. When you are ready to leave, thank the mermaid, and return yourself to waking consciousness.

Like the goddesses Venus and Aphrodite, the mermaid is connected with love and the moon. Go to the sea and throw flowers into the waves to solicit her help. Wear shells or the image of a mermaid when you are trying to attract a lover.

Two

Spriggan

The Image: The card shows three strange green spriggans with oversized heads scampering over a Cornish stone circle.

The Fairy: Spriggans are small, withered, ugly creatures with oversized heads, though they can inflate themselves when they want to be intimidating. They are dangerous Cornish fairies that steal from human houses, though they take a dim view of anyone trying to steal from the fairy folk. They guard the hidden treasure that is buried beneath the numerous prehistoric stones that are found scattered across the wild Cornish landscape.

One man tried to dig up the treasure in Trencrom Hill, but as he neared the gold, everything went dark, thunder crashed, and lightning streaked the sky. By its eerie light, he saw a large number of spriggans swarming out of the rocks. At first, they were small, but they swelled in size until they were as big as giants. The man managed to escape, but without his treasure. He was so shaken by his experience that he took to his bed and never worked again.[1]

Others who met the spriggans included a band of smugglers trying to bring their booty ashore near Long Rock. Three of them went to make arrangements for its disposal, while the other three rested and guarded the spoils. One of these, Tom Warren of Paul, heard music. He got up, intending to scare the intruders away, when he saw a band of tiny people all dressed in green with red caps. They were dancing and playing music. Tom laughed and shouted a rude greeting to them, but the dancers sprang up, suddenly armed with bows and arrows, spears, and slings. Alarmingly, they seemed to be getting bigger and bigger. Frightened now, Tom ran back to his mates, and they were all three forced to head out to sea in their small boat, bombarded by a hail of stones that burned like coals. No spriggans will touch salt water, so the men were safe enough in the sea, but they had to remain there until the dawn cockcrow forced the fairies to flee.

The name *spriggans* is derived from the Cornish *sperysyan*, meaning "spirit." Translated, the names of many fairies mean simply "spirit." Today's Cornish Pagans believe that the spriggans are the ancient guardian spirits of sacred sites, and warn that anyone damaging the ancient stone circles and holy places of Cornwall is liable to suffer the wrath of the spriggans.

In folklore, there is a general belief that buried treasure is guarded by spirits, either fairies, the ghosts of human dead, giants, or animals spirits.

Divinatory Meanings: The appearance of the ferocious and dishonest Spriggan in your cards points to theft, unscrupulous

methods, and dirty dealing, or perhaps the betrayal of princi-
ples or confidences.

Reversed Meanings: Appearing reversed in your spread, the spriggans are telling you that if you do not tackle your problems
head on, they will grow bigger and bigger until they are out of
all proportion.

Working with the Spriggan: Not recommended.

THREE

CHANGELING

The Image: The card shows a strange-looking baby with pointed ears. It is climbing out of a wooden cradle placed in the sunshine outside an old-fashioned, thatched cottage.

The Fairy: Fairies have been known to steal a human child and replace it with a changeling: a fairy baby or sometimes just a piece of wood that seems to be alive for a short time. Fairies of all nationalities kidnap human adults and children. The Welsh sometimes calls the whole fairy race *cipenapers*, which is just a contraction of "kidnappers."[2] Those most in danger of being snatched include women who have recently given birth, unbaptized babies, blond children, pretty girls, those sleeping beneath hawthorn bushes, and anyone wandering near fairy mounds at night.

Parents will soon realize that the baby in the crib is not their own, but a fairy surrogate. The changeling may have a withered or deformed appearance. It will probably be thin, weak, or ailing, and will cry continually. It may have a voracious appetite, be fond of dancing, be unnaturally precocious, or make some unguarded remark as to its age. In Ireland, all left-handed children are said to be changelings.

The method of discovering a changeling by means of eggshells is used in many places around the world. Empty eggshells are arranged around the hearth, and as the curious changeling gets up to examine them, he will peer into each, saying something like this: "This is but a windbag; I am so many hundred years old and I have never seen the likes of this." An alternative method is to go through the motions of brewing water in halves of eggshells. The changeling will reveal its ancient age by sitting up and declaring, "I have seen the egg before the hen, I have seen the acorn before the oak, but I have never seen brewing in an eggshell before!" It might even say, "I'm fifteen hundred years in the world and I've never seen a brewery of eggshells before!"[3]

When the changeling has been made to reveal its fairy nature, it will disappear up the chimney, and the real baby will be found alive and well at the door, or back in its cradle, sweetly sleeping.[4]

Parents would protect their children with pieces of iron placed beneath the cradles, crosses made from rowan wood and red thread, or St. John's wort, or the child might be wrapped in the father's shirt.

Divinatory Meanings: When the Changeling appears in the cards, it indicates that something, or someone, is not all it seems. The questioner may be the victim of fraud or duplicity.

Reversed Meanings: The Changeling reversed in your cards suggests that a younger person will surprise you with his or her insights into a situation. You would do well to listen to this person's advice.

Working with a Changeling: Not recommended.

Four

Banshee

The Image: The card shows two banshees: strange, white-faced women with red eyes. They stand on the bare branches of trees under the eerie light of a full moon.

The Fairy: Banshees can be heard weeping and wailing when a death or a disaster is about to occur. A banshee may look like a lovely, young maiden or she may appear as an ugly, old hag with eyes red from weeping. In some areas of Ireland, the banshee dresses in green; in others, she wears white; or yet again, she might be veiled and clad from head to foot in black. Banshees are usually seen in the moonlight, crouching in the dark or sitting in the branches of trees, combing their long hair, but beware: if one of these hairs should fall on you, it is a very bad omen indeed.

Every old Scots or Irish family has its own banshee, but the fairies only attach themselves to noble families of pure Milesian descent. The earliest written reference to a banshee was in Scotland in 1437, when a banshee foretold the death of James I of Scotland.

The Welsh have their own form of death omen called a Cyoerraeth. These creatures are sometimes heard but rarely seen, though they have long, black teeth, matted hair, withered arms, and wings. They tap on the windows of a dying person, groaning loudly.

Other death omens are the various beings called Washers at the Ford, who may be discovered washing the bloody garments of those about to die. In an ancient myth, the battle goddess Morrigan would sing on the eve of a battle and, in a stream, wash the entrails of those about to die. Those warriors who heard her spellbinding songs were destined to die in battle, while those who did not might have wit enough to live. Thus, her song is a herald of death, like the wail of the banshee, and this is probably the origin of banshee lore. In folklore, the Morrigan is sometimes deemed their leader and chooses the loveliest maidens to become banshees.

The word *banshee* is an anglicized form of the Gaelic *bean sidhe*, or *ban sith*, which simply means "woman fairy."

Divinatory Meanings: The Banshee brings you bad news or a warning of disaster. She is telling you that others are working behind the scenes to do you a disservice. Beware of evil gossip about you, and treachery by disloyal friends and loved ones.

Reversed Meanings: The Banshee appears reversed in your cards to advise you that your own psychic senses are developing at this time. Listen to your intuition, and trust your instincts. Take note of dreams, omens, and portents.

Working with a Banshee: Those families who possess banshees look upon them kindly, knowing that they simply warn of ill omen and do not cause it. However, none would dream of summoning a banshee, since ill fortune would inevitably follow her appearance.

FIVE

Fairy Horse/Kelpie

The Image: The upright card shows a fairy horse, its red color demonstrating that fire runs through its veins. Sparks fly from its hooves. The reversed card shows an ugly, gray-green kelpie, its muscles and bones clearly visible.

The Fairies: Fairy horses are very special creatures. They are made of fire and flame and are as swift as the wind. They are shod with silver and have golden bridles. They live for one hundred years, though sadly, it is possible that there are none left, as there is a legend that the last of them was owned by a lord of Connaught and was sold at his death. Refusing to be mounted by its baseborn buyer, it threw him to the ground and bolted, never to be seen again.[5]

Fairies like to ride horses, and occasionally shapeshift into them in order to trick the unwary into mounting them and then taking off on a wild, mischievous ride. Such fairies include the phooka, Robin Goodfellow, and boggarts.

Fairy horses have ready access to the Otherworld and may convey humans there, whether bodily or just in spirit. The Irish horse Aonbharr carried the hero Conan to the Otherworld, while Thomas the Rhymer was taken to the realm of the fairy by the milk-white steed of the elf queen. Tam Lin escaped from the fairy realm on a stolen white horse.

The Celts believed that the souls of the dead were taken to the Otherworld on horseback. Magicians and druids summoned magical horses or horse spirits to take them to Fairyland. In Greek myth, the horse of Otherworld journeying was Pegasos (Latin *Pegasus*), the horse of Apollo and the Muses. If a poet said, "I am mounting my Pegasus," he meant that he was inspired to write poetry. Many famous poets and musicians are said to have learned their craft in the Otherworld or the realm of the fairy, riding there on a mysterious fairy horse. A shaman's drum is often referred to as his "horse," since the drumbeat is the vehicle that enables him to travel to other realms.

• • •

The reverse of the card shows a fearsome kelpie, a Scottish water fairy who appears as a gray horse that encourages people to ride him. Once a person is astride, the kelpie will run off into the water, drown its passenger, and devour him, leaving only the entrails on the shore.

A kelpie at Corgarff in Aberdeen tricked a man who was trying to cross the swollen River Don. The beast offered to take him across, but halfway it submerged itself, dragging the man with him. However, the man managed to escape and the kelpie threw a boulder after him, which can still be seen and is known as "the Kelpie's Stone."

Kelpies are known to eat animals, humans, and other fairies that venture too close to their lairs. To see a kelpie is an omen of death or great misfortune. It is not always easy to spot a kelpie, however, since it is able to shapeshift into human form. One kelpie also appeared as an old woman and was put to bed by a group of girls. During the night he sucked the blood of all but one, who escaped over running water.[6] In this respect, the kelpie is a vampire.

Kelpies sometimes appear as men to seduce young women, but their hair always looks like seaweed or watercress. A handsome, young man courted one pretty girl, but when she discovered the seaweed and shells in his hair, she realized he was a fairy. He instantly turned into a horse and began to chase the girl in order to kill and eat her. He would have succeeded if she had not been saved by the appearance of a fairy bull.[7]

Divinatory Meanings (Fairy Horse): When the Fairy Horse appears upright in your cards, he indicates movement and travel, journeying to new places and new experiences. He is the harbinger of good health, vitality, energy, and innovation. Events will move quickly, and rapid progress will be made.

Reversed Meanings (Kelpie): If the Kelpie, rather than the Fairy Horse, appears upright in the cards, he heralds anxiety, impulsive behavior with bad consequences, misjudgment, hyperactivity, aggression, anger, and frustration.

Working with a Fairy Horse: The horse is a powerful creature, a symbol of the fertility of the land, and the power of the sun and the moon. The fairy horse has the ability to travel to all the different realms and is possibly the best guide to the Otherworld:

Relax. You find yourself at the center of a woodland, standing before a massive tree. Its branches seem to touch the sky, and you know that the roots will extend deep down into the Underworld. It is the World Tree that connects all the realms.

Tethered to it is a white horse, a powerful, beautiful steed. You are surprised to see that it has wings folded over its back.

You go forward and take the reins of the horse and climb onto its back. Its wings unfold and begin to beat powerfully.

If you wish to visit one of the realms of the Otherworld, the fairy horse will take you there. If you wish to visit some place in this world, then you may go there. The horse will take you wherever it is that you need to go at the moment, and show you what you need to learn.

When you are ready to return, thank the fairy horse, allow the scene to fade around you, and bring yourself back to waking consciousness.

Working with a Kelpie: Not recommended.

Six

TRYAMOUR

The Image: The card shows a lovely fairy maiden, dressed in gold. In the background is her human lover, a handsome knight.

The Fairy: According to one of the Arthurian legends, a knight called Launfal fell in love with a fairy maid.[8] She agreed to appear whenever he wished, on condition that he must never speak of her or summon her when others were present. Her name was Tryamour, meaning "test of love."

Guinevere noticed the young man and tried to seduce him. When he refused her advances, she exclaimed that he was not fit for a woman's love. He retorted that he was beloved of a lady whose lowliest handmaiden put the queen's beauty to shame. In saying this, he not only broke his promise to Tryamour, but also mortally insulted the queen. She complained to Arthur that Launfal had tried to rape her, and the knight was immediately arrested.

Though he argued his case well and persuaded most of the knights to side with him, it was decreed that he must produce his mistress within one year or die. Of course, the fairy would no longer come, and one year later, he stood in the courtyard at Camelot, waiting to be executed. Then through the gate, riding on a white horse, the fairy Tryamour appeared. All agreed that he had spoken truthfully; she was indeed the loveliest woman in existence.

The two lovers rode away together to Fairyland. The lady was never seen again, but Launfal appears once a year to look on the world of mortals that is now denied to him.

Divinatory Meanings: When Tryamour appears in your cards, she implies a choice of some kind. In this case, you are deciding with your heart, rather than your head. However, you should consider carefully, as all options have far-reaching consequences. If the card is well aspected (surrounded by helpful cards), it can point to harmony and true love. If it is badly aspected, it shows that a relationship will be tested to the breaking point.

Reversed Meanings: When Tryamour appears reversed in your cards, she indicates external and internal pressures on a relationship. You may experience contradictory feelings, inner conflicts, and indecision.

Working with Tryamour: Tryamour appeared solely for her lover Launfal.

THE LAKE MAIDEN

The Image: The card shows a fairy woman emerging from a still lake, bearing a shining sword. In the background, there is a waterfall; in the foreground, yellow water irises fringe the lake.

The Fairy: The Gwragedd Annwn are lovely fairy maidens who dwell beneath the lakes in the Black Mountains of Wales. They are exquisitely beautiful and sometimes come ashore to marry mortal husbands, bringing herds of fairy cows as dowries. They must never be touched with iron or struck, or they will return to the lake, taking their cattle with them.

    One legend says that the Lake Maidens were once human women who were turned into fairies by St. Patrick when he returned for a visit to Britain. They berated him for abandoning his native land for Ireland, and insulted him in no uncertain terms. Several old Welsh families claim descent from the Gwragedd Annwn.

Among the Arthurian legends is an account of such a fairy, titled the Lady of the Lake. She was a comely fairy who snatched the baby Lancelot from his real mother and disappeared with him into the depths of a lake. There, in her underwater kingdom, she tenderly raised him, preparing him for his role as Arthur's greatest knight. She also supplied Arthur with his magical sword Excalibur—a gift from the land of the fairy—which could not be bested in battle, and whose sheath safeguarded its owner from harm. As Arthur lay dying, he instructed Sir Bedivere to throw Excalibur into the lake. Though reluctant to part with the magical talisman, Sir Bedivere complied and was rewarded with the sight of an arm, clad in white samite, reaching up from the waters to clasp the sword. The Lady of the Lake took it back to the Otherworld to keep it until a hero arises who is worthy of bearing it.

In *Le Morte d'Arthur*, Thomas Mallory named the Lady of the Lake Nimue, but others have called her Niniane or Vivienne.[9] She was the daughter of Diones and the goddaughter of the goddess Diana. The archmagician Merlin saw her dancing in the forest and fell in love with her. Diana officiated at their marriage. Playing on his love for her, the Lady of the Lake persuaded Merlin to teach her all his magical secrets, after which she kept him a prisoner in an enchanted castle (or some say a cave or mound).

On the surface, this story seems like an act of betrayal, but it may have a deeper meaning. In Celtic lore, the initiate or poet is said to spend time in a glass or spiral castle in order to gain knowledge of the goddess' secrets of life and death.

Divinatory Meanings: The Lady of the Lake is the mistress of deep secrets and fairy magic. She reveals that there is a hidden power at work in your life, protecting and guiding you, equipping you with the tools to succeed.

Reversed Meanings: Appearing reversed, the Lake Maiden points out misplaced pride, false claims, and superficial knowledge mistaken for wisdom.

Working with the Lake Maiden: Water fairies have many powers, but the greatest one they possess is the gift of healing the mind, body, and spirit. Prepare yourself to visit the realm of the Lake Maiden in your imagination:

Relax. Imagine that you are walking along a lovely, secluded lake shore. It is warm and sunny. You hear the gentle sound of the water lapping.

A splash disturbs the surface of the water. Rising from it is a beautiful fairy, scattering crystal droplets of water. She holds out her arms to you.

You realize that she wants you to enter the water. Unafraid, you wade in and begin to swim in the cool water. She takes your hand and together you dive beneath the surface.

You are surprised to find that you can breathe the water just as easily as you normally breathe air. You enjoy the sensation of moving through the lake amid shoals of freshwater fish.

The Lake Maiden tugs on your hand and leads you to the entrance of an underwater cave. Swimming through, you find yourself surfacing in an underwater grotto. As you pull yourself from the water, you are aware of a peaceful, welcoming atmosphere.

The grotto is a gorgeous crystal cave. The walls are lined with brilliant, natural crystals that seem to be glowing with their own inner light. On a bed of white quartz lies a resplendent sword, the treasure of Albion that the Lady guards for its rightful possessor.

In the center of the cave is a fountain bubbling with pure, sparkling water. You go over to the fountain and drink some of the liquid. It is cold and clear. You feel it purifying your body. A deep, cleansing sensation fills you, and you feel all impurities drain away from your body into the sandy floor of the cave.

With her hand, the Lady strikes the crystal wall. Gradually you become aware that the crystals surrounding you have begun to hum. The pitch rises until they seem to vibrate and sing. You feel the vibration wash around you like warm water. It enters your body and fills you with healing energy. You feel whole. You feel at one with yourself.

When you have absorbed enough of the energy, allow the scene to fade around you, and return yourself to waking consciousness.

EIGHT

BOABHAN SITH

The Image: The Boabhan Sith appears against the hills of the Scottish Highlands. She looks like a pretty girl dressed in green with a plaid sash about her waist, but there is blood about her mouth. Poisonous mushrooms grow at her feet, and a crow flies in the sky nearby.

The Fairy: These Scottish Highland fairies look like beautiful women, but are really vampires thirsty for the blood of young men. In one tale, four callow friends went on a hunting trip and were forced to spend the night in an abandoned cottage. They lit a fire and set about making themselves cheerful, singing and dancing. One of them exclaimed that it would be more fun if there were some girls to dance with, and no sooner had he spoken than four young ladies appeared at the door. Delighted, three of the young men began to dance with them, while the fourth, a fine singer, supplied the accompaniment.

For a time, all was well, when suddenly the atmosphere changed and the dancing became wild and frenzied. As the dancers whirled, blood began to spatter the room. The horrified singer raced from the cottage and took refuge among the tethered horses. Soon the noises and screams issuing from the cottage died away, and the four fairies came out to look for the young man. For some reason they were unable to go among the horses—perhaps it was the iron horseshoes that kept them away—and the terrified man crouched there until the dawn cockcrow forced the fairies to flee. As he crept back into the cottage to discover what had become of his friends, a ghastly sight greeted him. The three men lay around the floor like broken dolls, stone dead and completely drained of blood.[10]

The term *boabhan sith* (pronounced "boh-van shee") is Scots Gaelic and means "wicked woman fairy." They appear first as crows or ravens, then as lovely girls in white or green dresses with plaid sashes, but with hooves instead of feet. Their wails can be heard for miles around. The term *boabhan* is sometimes used alone for a bad fairy or an unpleasant woman, a scold, or a hoodie crow. It is derived from the Irish Badbh, the fearsome war goddess who appears on the battlefield in the form of a crow to eat the flesh and drink the blood of fallen warriors.

In many parts of the world, including Britain and Ireland, several fairies have vampiristic tendencies and set out to suck the blood of humans. On the Isle of Man, it was believed that if water were not set out for them to drink, fairies would suck the blood of sleepers in the house. They might also bleed them and make a cake with the blood, and if the cake could not be found and eaten by the householders, they would waste away and die.[11] A large number of fairies try to seduce mortals in order to drain the strength and life force from them, or even suck their blood in the form of a classical vampire.

Many cultures held that blood was the animating spirit or life force (lose a lot of blood and you die), or even that the blood contained the soul. It was commonly thought that spirits are jealous of humankind's corporeal nature and are always hungry, and that blood could give them strength and form, at least temporarily.

Divinatory Meanings: When the Boabhan Sith appears in your cards, she heralds bad health, illness, energy drain, and a sense of oppression.

Reversed Meanings: When she appears reversed, the Boabhan Sith indicates self-pity, envy, negative thinking, depression, and self-obsession.

Working with a Boabhan Sith: Not recommended.

NINE

SELKIE

The Image: The card shows a woman emerging from the sea at sunset. She is a selkie who has shed her sealskin to become a woman. Other selkies about her retain their skins and remain seals.

The Fairy: Selkies are sea fairies found around the Orkney, Faeroe, and Shetland islands. Selkie means "seal," and these creatures are a common sight in these parts; the name Orkney is derived from the Norse *Orkneyjar*, meaning "Seal Islands." Sometimes the folk of the islands see human eyes staring back at them from the seals and know that these are no ordinary seals, but selkies.

Selkies take the form of seals in the sea, but when they come ashore, they shed their sealskins and assume human form. Some say they are bewitched humans who can come ashore on Midsummer Eve, locally called Johnsmas Eve, and cast off their sealskins and resume their true shape. Others say that they are fairies and can only take a human shape at certain times; some say this is every Midsummer, others that it is every ninth night. Some believe that they are the spirits of the drowned.

One thing is for certain: they choose lonely places for their transformation, being shy and gentle creatures. Once in human form, the selkie folk will dance together under the moonlight or sun themselves on the rocks. They hide their discarded sealskins carefully, since without them they cannot return to the sea. Many unscrupulous human men have tried to get themselves a selkie bride, creeping up as the selkie folk rest, and stealing a skin.

One old story tells of a man who was not interested in any of the island girls, but dreamed of a fairy love. The old folks said he would come to a bad end, but eventually he was able to steal a sealskin and marry a selkie maid. Together they had three children, but the selkie girl was always distant and spent long hours gazing longingly at the sea. Her husband had hidden her magical sealskin, however, so she could not return to the water. Then one day the children were playing with an old sea chest. At the bottom lay a strange, gray cloak made of skin. They excitedly ran to their mother, crying, "Mother, mother! What is this?" Recognizing it immediately, she seized the sealskin and ran to the shore. Her husband and children never saw her again. The man pined away and died of a broken heart.

There are handsome male selkies, too, and the local women find them very seductive. Island men who do not keep their wives satisfied risk their wives taking selkie lovers! A woman who wanted a selkie lover might go to the sea at high tide and drop seven tears in the water. Any girl who went missing after walking on the seashore was known to have gone away with the selkies.

However, male selkies are not always friendly. They can cause sudden storms that wreck boats and drown fishermen.

Divinatory Meanings: The Selkie indicates the ability to adapt to any situation and any environment. Her lesson is a balanced approach, and the need for fluidity, movement, and good co-ordination.

Reversed Meanings: The Selkie reversed indicates dissatisfaction with a situation, but the lack of any means to resolve it. All attempts at change will be frustrated, and a stalemate ensues.

Working with a Selkie: You can take a journey with the selkie folk by using the power of your imagination:

Relax. Imagine that you are standing on the seashore. It is twilight and a reddish light fills the sky and falls over the white-tipped waves of the sea.

In the sea you can see several gray seals heading toward the shore. As they reach it, their flippers become hands, their black eyes assume human intelligence, and, shedding their sealskin cloaks, they stand up as human men and women. They are slim and restless folk, seemingly very shy. You stay quiet, hoping not to frighten them.

Eventually they are reassured and take you by the hand to run and dance along the beach, darting in and out of the waves.

After a while, they indicate that they are about to return to the ocean, and invite you to go with them. One of them lends you a sealskin cloak—a great gift. As you put it around your shoulders, you feel yourself shrinking. This is not frightening, but quite a pleasant sensation. Your hands become flippers and your legs a tail.

A wave washes you into the water, and to your delight, you find yourself swimming with the ease of a seal. With your new friends, you play in the waves. Spend as long as you like enjoying this sensation, learning what it is to be a creature of earth and of water.

When you wish to leave, return to the shore. Your flippers become hands, and you remove the sealskin cloak. You feel your body return to its usual shape, though it has a new suppleness and strength. You give the sealskin cloak to the waiting selkie and thank her. With a grin she throws it about her and dives into the sea.

Allow yourself to return to waking consciousness.

MORGAN LE FAY

THE LADY OF THE AUTUMN COURT
MORGAN LE FAY

The Image: The card shows Morgan le Fay, a tall, red-haired woman dressed in a red gown and holding a sword. She is surrounded by apple trees, which bear blossom and fruit at the same time. In the background is the magical island of Avalon, which she rules as its queen. A butterfly perches in the corner of the card.

The Fairy: Morgan le Fay ("Morgan the Fairy") was the sister of King Arthur. In his stories, Thomas Mallory made her the wife of Urien and the mother of Yvain. She was a rather tempestuous, malefic woman who tried to murder both her husband and King Arthur, and who had a number of lovers.[12] She learned the magical arts from Merlin and used this knowledge to trick Arthur into sleeping with her. From this union she bore Mordred, the son who brought discord to Camelot and died inflicting a fatal wound on his father.

But these tales are of a late date. Earlier tradition makes her the ruler of the island of Avalon. Some associate Avalon with modern-day Glastonbury in England. Its name is derived from the Welsh *afall*, meaning "apple" (*aball* in Irish), since the island is covered in apple orchards. It is also sometimes called the Fortunate Isle and may be compared with the Irish Tir Nan Og (Fairyland).

Avalon is inhabited by nine sisters, of which Morgan is the most beautiful and most powerful. As King Arthur lay dying after the battle of Camlann, Morgan appeared with a ship of women and carried Arthur to the island of Avalon. There he still lies with his knights under a fairy hill until Britain shall need him again. The island existed in legend long before the familiar Arthurian tales. In early Celtic legend, it could only be reached on a boat guided by the sea god Barinthus, and was a place fit only for the bravest and best.[13]

Morgan was a goddess of the druids, perhaps related to Modron or Matrona, the Welsh divine mother goddess. She has aspects of maiden, mother, and crone. She is certainly related to the Lady of the Lake and to the fairy rulers of enchanted islands. Her name may be derived from the Welsh *môr*, "sea," and *gân*, "a birth," i.e., "born of the sea." Again, the name may arise from the Welsh *Mor Gwyn*, meaning "white lady."

Divinatory Meanings: Morgan le Fay is the mistress of occult knowledge. She indicates wisdom and power gained from study and experience combined. Depending on the surrounding cards, she may indicate aspiration and ambition, but also cunning and ruthlessness.

She may represent a real woman in your life: an independent woman who covets success; who is passionate, sensual, and fond of possessions and pleasure, but also capable of being manipulative and controlling.

Reversed Meanings: When Morgan le Fay appears reversed in your spread, you find yourself in a situation beyond your control. Others are orchestrating events, and for now you will just have to go along with them until an opportunity to express your desires and exert your will presents itself.

Morgan le Fay reversed in your cards may represent a real woman in your life: she is vain and selfish, a woman who desires power over others, and will go to great lengths to get it.

Working with Morgan le Fay: You may visit the realm of Morgan le Fay in your imagination by using the following pathworking:

Relax. Imagine that you are standing on the edge of a lake. An eerie mist covers the water and you cannot see for more than a few yards. Even the birds are quiet.

You become aware of the sound of a gentle splashing. Slowly, a stately boat glides into view. It crests through the water as if by magic and comes to rest on the shore before you. It is made of silver and has a moon-white sail. In it sits a noble-looking woman, clad all in red. Her hair is also red and flows long and sleek down her back. She holds out her hand to you, and you step into the boat.

The boat starts to move silently through the gossamer threads of mist that shroud the lake. Your companion is quiet, but smiles gently at you.

Eventually your magic barge comes to rest beside a jetty made from snow-white wood, and you step ashore to find yourself on a lovely island. Though the mists hide it from the mortal world, the island is lit by bright sunshine. It is covered by orchards of apple trees that bear drifts of blossoms, which the gentle breeze scatters, creating a snowstorm of soft petals. Among the branches hang mature fruit, round golden apples, full and ripe.

Morgan le Fay—for your hostess is none other—hands you a beautiful apple and invites you to taste it. You bite into it, and it is so sweet and juicy that your mouth waters. You feel the fruit fill you with a wild power. Morgan tells you that whoever eats the fruit of the Otherworld can never be the same again. Now you are part fairy yourself and can return to her realm whenever you wish.

You may stay here as long as you like, speaking with Morgan le Fay. She knows all the secrets of magic and herbs, and may share some of these with you.

When you are ready to return, thank your hostess, and take the magic barge back to the shore of the human realm.

Allow yourself to return to normal waking consciousness.

The Knave of the Autumn Court

Phooka

The Image: The card shows a strange, hairy being with a goat's head.

The Fairy: This Irish goblin can appear as a goat, horse, dog, bull, or eagle. He is always black with blazing eyes and usually has something of the goat about him, often a goat head or hooves. The Irish poet Yeats, who recorded many fairy traditions, speculated that his name may be derived from *poc*, which means "he-goat."[14] The term *phooka* is often used to refer to the devil, and "playing the phooka" means "playing the devil," i.e., being wicked.[15]

The Irish call Halloween "Phooka Night." After this time, the Phooka blights any crops remaining in the fields and makes the blackberries unfit to eat,[16] a service performed by the devil in France.

In his horse form, the Phooka offers rides to weary travelers, then takes off at a mad pace, before dumping them in a ditch and galloping away laughing. This tendency is illustrated in the tale of Morty Sullivan, who, at the age of fourteen, ran away to sea. Many years later, he returned home to visit his parents, but discovered that they had been dead for some years. Repenting the neglect of his loving family, he determined to go on a pilgrimage to the chapel of St. Gobnate in a wild, mountainous place called Ballyvourney.

With a pious zeal, he set off immediately, but had not gone far when evening fell. There was no moon to guide his steps, and a dense fog began to surround him. Within no time at all, he was completely lost. Suddenly Morty saw a light before him and piously thought that the saint had sent it to guide him to the shrine, but however quickly he walked to try to overtake it, the light seemed to get further and further away. He struggled on over the rough countryside for many miles.

Just as he was about to collapse with fatigue, the light finally seemed to get nearer. He was surprised to discover that it was actually a fire, beside which sat an old woman. This puzzled and frightened him, especially when he saw that the woman's eyes were a blazing red. After watching him in silence for a while, she sharply demanded his name.

"Morty Sullivan, at your service," he replied.

"We'll soon see about that!" she cried, her eyes turning a pale green. She told Morty that she would take pity on him and lend him a horse to complete his journey. No sooner had she spoken than a jet-black horse appeared. The old hag bundled Morty onto its back, and the horse suddenly bolted away, tearing over precipices, barging through torrents, rushing head-long through the mountains. The next morning, some pilgrims discovered Morty flat on his back under a steep cliff, black-and-blue from his ride on the Phooka. He swore on the spot never to take a quart of whiskey on a pilgrimage with him again.[17]

When he is not bruising and battering travelers with wild rides, the Phooka can be friendly, and if he is well treated, he will help farmers and millers. One day, Phadrig fell asleep in an old mill, and when he awoke, he was astounded to see six little fairies and an old man in tattered clothing who directed them to mill the corn. He felt sorry for the old Phooka in his tattered clothes, so one day he bought a fine silk suit and laid it out on the floor of the mill. The delighted Phooka put it on and declared that he was now a fine gentleman and would grind the corn no more.[18]

Divinatory Meanings: When the Phooka appears in a spread, he betokens childishness, insolence, immaturity, an inability to deal with authority, and a lack of self-control.

He may indicate a real person in the life of the questioner: an unreliable, lazy young man who is amiable, a dreamer, easily led or discouraged, and possibly a liar.

Reversed Meanings: The Phooka reversed may point to a real person in the life of the questioner: a young man who is hard working, methodical, and patient, but a plodder rather than quick and clever. He is loyal and trustworthy, and slow to anger, but implacable when aroused.

The reversed card may be telling you that if you get carried away with wild flights of fancy, you may lose what is beneath your nose. Patience and steady effort are needed.

Working with the Phooka: Not recommended.

THE QUEEN OF THE AUTUMN COURT

QUEEN OONAGH

The Image: The card shows a gorgeous fairy woman clad in glittering silver, with long, golden hair. She stands before a fairy hill at sunset.

The Fairy: Oonagh, or Una, is Queen of the Western Fairies of Ireland, and the wife of King Finvarra. She is more beautiful than any woman of the earth.[19] Her golden hair sweeps the ground, and she is robed in silver gossamer, glittering as if with diamonds, though they are dewdrops that sparkle all over it. She lives in Knockshegouna, "the fairy mound of Oonagh," east of Lough Derg.

Oonagh appears in one late tale as the wife of the Fin MacCool.[20] Fin was a mighty man, but he became worried when he heard that a giant called Cucullin wanted to fight him to prove himself the better warrior. Cucullin, it was rumored, was so strong and powerful that he carried around a thunderbolt that he had flattened into a pancake with his bare hands. Oonagh, who was part fairy, told him not to worry his head, as she would help him.

Taking nine threads of different colors, she plaited three braids with three colors in each. She put one around her right arm, one around her heart, and the third around her right ankle, for then she knew that nothing could fail her. Next she kneaded twenty-one cakes of bread, hiding iron griddles in twenty of them, and baked them in the fire. Lastly, she took a pot of milk and made curds and whey, instructing Fin what to do with them.

It was Fin's peculiar gift that he could put his thumb in his mouth and thereby have a great many things revealed to him. By this method, he divined that Cucullin would arrive at two o'clock that afternoon. Furthermore, it was revealed that all the strength Cucullin possessed lay in the middle finger of his right hand. If he should lose that, then he would be no more than an ordinary man.

As the time of Cucullin's arrival approached, Oonagh made up a giant cradle and bade Finn to lie down in it, covering him up with baby blankets and telling him that he must pretend to be his own child.

As expected, Cucullin arrived at two o'clock, knocking on the door and asking whether this was where the great Finn lived. Oonagh politely asked him in and bade him be seated, apologizing for the absence of her husband. "He has left home in a great rage, looking for some buffoon called Cucullin who wants to fight him. I hope he doesn't find him or he will tear him to pieces!"

"I am Cucullin and I have been looking for Fin for twelve months or more!" the giant exclaimed.

At this Oonagh laughed and looked at Cucullin scornfully. "Did you ever set eyes on Fin?" she asked. Cucullin shook his head. "I thought not," said Oonagh, "for you are a poor-looking creature and he will make mincemeat of you. Never mind, I wonder if you would be good enough to turn the house for me, for there is no one to do it with Fin away."

Cucullin was startled, but agreed. He went outside, cracked his middle finger and picked up the house, turning it around on its foundations. Seeing this, Fin, tucked up in his crib, broke into a sweat, but Oonagh seemed undaunted. She turned to Cucullin and said that the spring had run dry and that Fin had intended to pull apart some rocks behind the hill, since there was water behind them. Would he mind doing that little job for her, since her man was away?

Cucullin set off and was somewhat surprised to see a solid cliff face below him. Nevertheless, he cracked his middle finger and tore a cleft in the rock, four hundred feet deep. Seeing this, Fin began to quake in his boots, but Oonagh seemed calm enough.

"Well," she said, "you had better come along in and have a bite to eat." She set before him the loaves that she had baked, a churn of butter, half a side of bacon, and a pile of cabbage. Cucullin took a huge bite from one of the loaves, then cried in anguish that it had broken two of his teeth!

"My goodness," said Oonagh, "I forgot to tell you that this is Fin's bread, and that only he can eat it, he and that little child in the cradle there." So saying, she gave the one good loaf to Fin, who gobbled it down. Cucullin looked amazed and began to think he was lucky not to meet the father if this was but the child.

"Get up, my lovely, and show this Cucullin something that wouldn't shame your father," Oonagh called to Fin. Accordingly, he got out of the cradle and said to Cucullin, "Are you strong enough to squeeze water out of a white stone?" Cucullin seized a stone, but try as he might, he could get no water from it.

"You poor creature!" exclaimed Fin, "I'll show you what Fin's infant son can do, and you can imagine the might of the father!" So saying, he took the stone and slyly exchanged it for the curds, squeezing them until the whey ran out. "And now," he said, "I am away back to my cradle, for I won't waste time with a man who cannot eat my father's bread or squeeze water from a little stone. You'd best be away before my father comes home, for he'll squash you flat in two minutes!"

Cucullin decided that the child was right, and that he had better make himself scarce in Fin's part of the country. "Before you go," he said to Fin, "let me feel what kind of teeth are able to eat bread like that."

Fin agreed and opened his mouth. "They are quite far back," Oonagh prompted, "so you will need to put you hand right in his mouth." Cucullin obligingly put his fingers further into Fin's mouth, and grasping the opportunity, Fin bit down hard, severing Cucullin's famous middle finger, leaving him weak as a mortal man. And it was all thanks to the wisdom of Oonagh that Fin was able to defeat Cucullin.[21]

Divinatory Meanings: When Queen Oonagh appears in the cards, she indicates the development of practical skills, finding solutions to practical problems, help, good advice, and friendship.

The card may betoken a real woman in the life of the questioner: a woman who is clever and shrewd, practical, and helpful, with a great deal of common sense.

Reversed Meanings: When the Queen of the Autumn Court appears reversed in a spread, she indicates overwhelming feelings, mood swings, emotional instability, the overestimating of problems, and a refusal to contemplate solutions.

The reversed card may also indicate a real woman who is unreliable, untrustworthy, unstable, hysterical, and perverse.

Working with Oonagh: The witches of the past learned their magic from the fairies, meeting with them in the woodlands and fairy mounds that ordinary people avoided. During the Burning Times, many witches admitted to visiting the Fairy Queen and her train, to be given herbs, potions, and the secrets of the Craft. If you wish, you can meet the Queen of the Fairies by taking a journey in your imagination:

Relax. You are in the woodlands, following a path deep into the heart of the greenwood. It is twilight, and a purple light shadows the forest floor.

As you go deeper, you become aware of a white light ahead of you and the gentle murmur of quiet voices. Then, as you round a bend in the path, you see a truly magical sight.

Before you stands the Queen of the Fairies, Oonagh. She is dressed entirely in white, and her dress sparkles with the reflection of a thousand dewdrops. Her golden hair sweeps the ground, and her skin is as white as snow. Her lips are like two rubies pressed together, and her eyes like cornflowers on a summer morning. Her laughter is like the tinkling of a silver bell, and her voice as sweet as a nightingale's. She shines with an inner radiance. You have never seen anything so beautiful.

Around her are her attendant fairies. Some are small, some are large, some are stately knights, others are like small children, and some are lovely maidens, but none are as lovely as Oonagh herself.

She smiles at you and invites you to join them. You bow to her politely and sit among the fairies at her feet. You can just enjoy being here, or you can speak to Oonagh if you think she would welcome it. If you are especially honored, she may give you a gift from Fairyland.

When you are ready to return, thank the fairy queen, and walk back through the woods.

Return yourself to waking consciousness.

The King of the Autumn Court
King Finvarra

The Image: The card shows a handsome, mature fairy king sitting before a chessboard in his magnificent palace, which lies beneath a fairy mound.

The Fairy: Finvarra is the king of the *daoine sidhe* ("People of Peace") of the west or Connacht in Ireland, and is called the Fairy King of Ulster.[22] He keeps friendly relations with the best families of Galway, especially the Kirwans of Castle Hacket, who always leave out a keg of Spanish wine for him at night. In return, the wine cellars at the castle are never empty.

His fairy abode is beneath Knockma Hill, and his name, which means "white topped," may be an adjective applied to the hill.[23] He sometimes abducts mortal women and takes them there, as the following tale illustrates:

Once a great lord had a beautiful wife called Ethna, whom he adored. One evening, while attending a feast in her honor, she suddenly fainted. Alarmed servants carried her to her room, but she could not be woken until the morning. She declared that she had spent the night in a beautiful palace and longed to sleep and go there again in her dreams. When the evening came, low music was heard outside, and she again fell into a deep trance. Her old nurse was set to watch her, but fell asleep herself, and when she awoke, the young bride was gone. A search was made, but no sign of her could be found.

The young lord decided to go to Knockma to ask for the help of the fairy king Finvarra. However, as he approached the mound, he heard a voice inside saying, "Happy is Finvarra, for now he has the lovely bride in his palace, and she will never see her husband again." Astounded, he listened more closely and heard another voice reply, "Yes, but if he only knew that he would find her should he dig into the center of the hill!" The young lord immediately sent for workers to dig into the fairy mound.

The workmen made good progress and dismantled a good part of the hill, but as darkness fell, they decided to stop for the night and continue in the morning. The next day, all the soil was back in the hill again. Determined, they started again and only stopped when it was too dark to see. The next morning, all the earth was back again. This went on for three days and the lord was near despair, when a voice whispered to him:

"Sprinkle the earth you have removed with salt, and all will be well." This he did, and they were able to dig deep into the hill. If they put their ears to the ground, they could hear music and voices. Then they heard Finvarra himself say, "Stop your work, and at sunset I shall give the bride back to her husband." They stopped, and at sunset the young lord saw his wife walking toward him along the path. He happily clasped her in his arms, and together they rode home to the castle.

Sadly, his joy was short-lived. Ethna lay with her eyes closed and never spoke a word, or smiled, or gave any sign that she knew where she was. Everyone grew sad and realized that she must have eaten fairy food. After this had gone on for a year, a voice was heard to say, "Though her body is present, her spirit is still with the fairies." Another voice added, "She will remain so forever unless her husband breaks the spell. The girdle about her waist is fastened with an enchanted pin. He should unloose it, then burn the girdle and throw its ashes before the door, and bury the enchanted pin. Only then will her spirit return from the sidhe."

The young lord hastily carried out these mysterious instructions, burying the pin beneath a fairy thorn. Only then did Ethna's soul return to her body, and the couple was truly reunited. She remembered her time in the realm of the sidhe as no more than a dream. The deep cut in the Knockma hill remains to this day and is called "the Fairy's Glen."[24]

It seems likely that Finvarra may once have been a god of the dead or underworld, with some functions as a vegetation spirit, since he is deemed to have the power of bringing good harvests.

Divinatory Meanings: When the Fairy King Finvarra appears in your spread, he indicates authority and authority figures, government, the law, legal settlements, contracts, and agreements.

The card may indicate a real person in the questioner's life: a mature man who is concerned with social issues and people, and is compassionate, sensitive, and emotionally supportive.

Reversed Meanings: The reversed card indicates self-indulgent sensuality, clandestine love affairs, a lack of self-control, selfishness, or using other people without caring about their needs and feelings.

The reversed card may indicate a real person in your life: a moody, languid man who is lecherous, unscrupulous, disloyal, and perhaps even violent.

Working with King Finvarra: You can visit King Finvarra by taking a journey in your imagination:

Relax. It is a clear autumn evening, and you find yourself in a fine green meadow. In its center stands an old fairy mound, a hump that stands as high as your head. It is covered with grass, harebells, and daisies.

As the evening light fades, you become aware that lights are filtering out from tiny holes within the mound. You put your ear to it, and you can hear strains of delightful music—a soulful lament played on a harp. But try as you might, you cannot find an entrance to the mound.

You seat yourself upon it, with your face pressed into the grass, the better to hear the fairy music emanating from it. You can hear the sounds of sweet voices and laughter within.

Gradually, you become aware that you are not alone. Sitting beside you, with an amused smile on his face, is a stately male fairy. You know him to be Finvarra, King of the Sidhe.

Though this is not the time for you to enter the fairy mound, he welcomes you on behalf of the fairy folk and names you "Fairy Friend."

You can spend some time talking with King Finvarra, listening to the fairy music, feeling it entering your soul and changing your forever.

When you are ready to return, bid farewell to the fairy king, and return yourself to waking consciousness.

1. Robert Hunt, *Popular Romances of the West of England* (1881; reprint, Chatto and Windus, 1930).

2. K. M. Briggs, *The Fairies in Tradition and Literature* (London: Routledge & Kegan Paul, 1967).

3. Crofton Croker, *Fairy Legends and Traditions of the South of Ireland* (London: John Murray, 1826).

4. Ibid.

5. Ibid.

6. J. F. Campbell, *Popular Tales of the Western Highlands Orally Collected* (1890).

7. Ibid.

8. B. de Roquefort, ed., *Lanval: Poësies de Marie de France* (Paris: 1920).

9. Thomas Mallory, *Le Morte d'Arthur* (1485).

10. www.mysteriousbritain.co.uk/folklore.

11. Lady Wilde, *Ancient Legends, Mystic Charms and Superstitions of Ireland* (London: Ward & Downey, 1887).

12. Thomas Mallory, *Morte d'Arthur* (1485).

13. Mike Dixon-Kennedy, *Celtic Myth and Legend* (London: Blandford, 1997).

14. W. B. Yeats, *Folk and Fairy Tales of the Irish Peasantry* (1888).

15. Crofton Croker.

16. W. B. Yeats, *Folk and Fairy Tales of the Irish Peasantry* (1888).

17. Adapted from Crofton Croker, *Fairy Legends and Traditions of the South of Ireland* (London: John Murray, 1826).

18. Adapted from Lady Wilde, *Ancient Legends, Mystic Charms and Superstitions of Ireland* (London: Ward & Downey, 1887).

19. Lady Wilde, ibid.

20. Though the characters have the names of ancient gods and heroes, in this late folktale their characters and relationships have changed somewhat from the original.

21. W. B. Yeats, *Fairy Tales of Ireland* (London: Harper Collins, 1990).

22. Lady Wilde, ibid.

23. Ronan Coghlan, *Handbook of Fairies* (Capall Bann, 1998).

24. Adapted from Lady Wilde, *Ancient Legends, Mystic Charms and Superstitions of Ireland* (1887).

The Winter Court

Ace

Knocker

The Card: The card shows the old engine-house of an abandoned Cornish tin mine, circled by a raven. Before it are four knockers: small, dark fairies that normally live inside the mine. They carry lamps and mining tools and are dressed in shirts and waistcoats.

The Fairy: Knockers live in the tin mines of Devon and Cornwall in the southwest of England. They are small, ugly, and thin-limbed, with hook noses and mouths like slits, which stretch from ear to ear. Though all the mines are now closed, the fairies once guided miners to good mineral seams by tapping, or "knocking," in return for food, traditionally a bit of

Cornish pasty. However, they were not always helpful and would sometimes try to frighten the miners by making faces at them or performing grotesque dances. They were offended by whistling and swearing, and would punish these misdemeanors with bad luck or a harmless shower of stones.

Some knockers, however, are positively malevolent. The knockers at the Chaw ("Raven") Gulley on Dartmoor are particularly vicious. A raven warns them whenever anyone tries to enter the mine to hunt for the treasure that is buried there, and they will kill the intruder by cutting the rope the man uses to lower himself into the shaft. His body will be found laid out on the surface the next day.

The Welsh equivalents of knockers are *coblynau* or *koblernigh*. These work in coal mines, rather than tin mines, tapping to indicate good coal seams. The word *coblyn* means both "knocker" and "sprite." Though the coblynau are sometimes spotted working on coal faces themselves, they do not actually mine anything, they are just pretending.[1]

Our ancestors knew that most of their precious jewels came from beneath the ground, and that these were guarded by spirits that live in the earth. Practically every culture in the world has stories of these fairies, who often dressed as miners, with miniature picks, lamps, and hammers. All the metals and minerals of the earth belong to them. When miners venture into these Underworld realms, they encounter spirits who may either aid or hinder them, according to how they behave themselves. If they honor the spirits, usually by leaving offerings in the form of food, the fairies may lead favored miners to rich seams. Those who show a lack of respect are punished with showers of stones.

Divinatory Meanings: Knockers and other mine fairies are the guardians of the earth's riches, and this card concerns your material wealth. The appearance of the Knocker in your spread indicates financial or material gain and the establishing of a firm foundation in some practical matter.

Reversed Meanings: The Knocker card reversed in your spread hints at financial loss, bad investments, money troubles, or difficulties with property. The card reversed may mean a poor attitude toward money, leading to either profligacy or miserliness.

Working with an Earth Elemental: Earth elementals (of which the knockers are but one form) rule the element of earth. In magic, earth is concerned with material things and practical matters, health, and wealth. To invoke an earth elemental to help you with these concerns, make an incense composed of half a teaspoon fir needles, three teaspoons pine wood, a few drops of patchouli oil, half a teaspoon clover flowers, one teaspoon pine resin, and half a teaspoon primrose flowers. Burn a pinch of this incense on a charcoal block and say, "Ye Creatures of Earth, I implore you to come to me, and to aid me in my work."

Close your eyes and relax. Imagine that you find yourself in a landscape at night, curtained by trees. Before you is a valley within a mountainous landscape. Through the trees, seemingly from the earth itself, appears the elemental of the earth. Take note of his or her appearance and tell him or her your name. Ask for help with practical skills, if you wish. Spend as much time with the creature as you need. When you are ready to leave, thank the elemental, and return yourself to waking consciousness.

To please the fairies, you should remember that the earth's resources are all precious; they should not be wasted or exploited by greed. In all situations, take only what you need and no more.

Two

TROW

The Card: A squat, misshapen fairy, dressed entirely in gray, creeps along a misty landscape on a Shetland island. Three golden coins are shown in the border of the card.

The Fairy: Trows are known in the Shetland and Orkney Islands, where they are also called Night Stealers or Night Creepers. They are squat and misshapen, with wild hair and sallow faces; they dress entirely in gray to blend in with the misty landscape. They are smaller than most human men. Trows are never seen in daylight, but go out during the hours of darkness to visit the islander's cottages as soon as the humans have gone to bed. They like to warm themselves by the fire and are mortally offended to find a locked door keeping them out. To this day, islanders leave their houses and possessions unlocked so as not to anger the trows.

Trows live inside the old burial mounds, or sometimes caves, where they keep their gold, silver, and precious jewels. Inside the mounds, they hold great feasts and are especially fond of music and dancing. Sometimes trows invite humans into their mounds, especially gifted musicians. They rewarded one fiddler with a magical trowie shilling, so that no matter how many times he spent it, it always found its way back to his pocket. However, the silly man boasted of this gift, and the trowie shilling vanished forever. The trows' great festivals are Yule and Midsummer, when they leave the mounds and can be seen performing a lopsided crouching-and-hopping dance called *henking*.

Trows kidnap human children and leave changelings— sickly looking trowlings—in their place. Even now, islanders will refer to someone who looks pale and ill as "trowie." One fisherman saw a number of trows scurrying in the direction of his brother-in-law's house, where his sister lay in labor. He realized that they were about to steal the new baby. Rushing to the door, he turned the iron key in the lock. The furious trows, cheated of their prize, bewitched him, robbing him of the power to move. He remained in this position for many hours until an old woman passed by and blessed him, and the curse was lifted.

The term *trow* is possibly derived from the Scandinavian *troll*, meaning "bewitch." The Norse influence is strong in the islands, and most of the islanders have Viking blood.

Divinatory Meanings: When the Trow creeps into your spread, someone is taking advantage of your good nature. People who will make no effort on their own behalf are abusing your generosity. This may refer to friends or relatives who impose on you, borrow from you without repaying the loan, expect you to pay for everything, or take up all your precious time and attention. Inconsiderate guests may outstay their welcome and abuse your hospitality.

Reversed Meanings: The Trow card reversed indicates that if you do not take care of something and recognize its true value, you will lose it or it will be taken from you. An interesting offer or a gift may be withdrawn if you gossip or boast about it.

Working with the Trow: Not recommended.

THREE

BOGGART

The Card: The card shows a horrible, hairy boggart skulking along a deserted lane at night. It has long, yellow, pointed teeth and yellow eyes. The waning moon is a mere sliver in the dark sky.

The Fairy: Boggarts are most common in northwest England and Scotland and are occasionally called barguests, trashes, or shrikers, the latter name earned from their horrible cries. If it chooses, a boggart may appear as a white cow or horse, a white or black dog, or in human form. In their natural state, boggarts are dark and hairy, with long, yellow teeth.

Some say that boggarts are brownies who have turned evil. They may wreck houses, steal children's suppers, break valuable possessions, and hide things. A single boggart can terrorize a whole neighborhood. They eat wood and are able to consume a whole house. If a family tries to move away from them, they will climb into the crocks and butter churns and travel with the unfortunate people to their new home.[2]

One particular boggart haunted the country lanes around Longridge in Lancashire. From behind, it looked like a harmless old woman in a fringed shawl and poke bonnet, but when she turned around, she would reveal that the bonnet was empty and her head was in the basket she carried. The head would shriek with laughter and snap at the unfortunate victim.

However, there is an account of a Lincolnshire farmer who managed to get the better of a boggart. One day, the farmer bought a new piece of land that adjoined his own and went to inspect it, only to find that a great, hairy boggart claimed the land as his. After some argument, they decided to share the crop equally, and the farmer asked the boggart whether he would like the part that grew above ground, or the part that grew below ground. The boggart thought about it and decided to settle on the part that grew above ground.

The farmer proceeded to plant potatoes, and when the boggart came along for his share, he got nothing but useless tops. The boggart was extremely angry, but an agreement was an agreement. He swore not to be fooled again, and said that next season he would have what grew below ground. The following year, there was a lovely crop of corn, and the boggart was left with useless stubble. Now the boggart was hopping mad and insisted that the following year the farmer should plant wheat again, and that they should harvest the field together, each one starting at either end and each one keeping what they harvested. Since a boggart is much stronger than a man is, he reckoned he'd have the advantage.

Dejectedly, the farmer returned home, unhappy that he would have to go to all the work of planting and caring for the crop, only to lose most of it to the lazy boggart who did nothing. In the end, he decided to consult a cunning man, the seventh son of a seventh son. He came away from this visit very pleased, having been advised to plant thin iron rods in the ground at the boggart's end of the field. The day of harvesting arrived, and both set to work with their sickles. The stupid boggart couldn't figure out why his work was so hard and why his sickle kept getting blunted. He looked at the farmer at the opposite end of the field, swinging away merrily and making good progress. At last he stood up and screeched that the farmer could have the bloody field. He would have nothing more to do with it.[3]

Divinatory Meanings: When the Boggart appears in your cards, he indicates that there will be trouble or some disturbance at home. There may be family arguments, quarrels, and disruptions, perhaps involving a troublesome child or teenager.

Reversed Meanings: The Boggart card reversed indicates that to succeed in gaining your ends, you will need to be clever and tactful when dealing with others. Your diplomatic skills and cunning will be tested to the utmost.

Working with a Boggart: Not recommended.

FOUR

GRIM

The Card: The card shows a hooded fairy dressed in black, carrying a scythe. Look closely and you will see that it is a skeleton. It wanders among the gravestones of a churchyard while mist rises about its feet.

The Fairy: Grim is a common name among English fairies; a Fairy Grim appeared in the famous *Life of Robin Goodfellow*, written in 1628. The fact that the name was once very widespread is evidenced by the number of English place names with *grim* in them, such as Grim's Dyke and Grimley (meaning "grove of the goblin"). The name is often used in relation to those ancient earthworks that are associated with fairies in folklore; there is a Grim's Ditch in Wiltshire and a Grim's Dyke in Hampshire, among many others.

The name Grim is derived from Grimr, one of the titles of the god Odin, or Woden. It means "masked one," or "hooded one," as the god was often known to go about in disguise among mortals as Grimr, perhaps appearing as a poor man or a shipwrecked sailor. He would reward or punish humans according to how they treated him. Many English fairies are similarly hooded or have *hood* as part of their name.

The Fairy Grim is a herald of death and misfortune, as this old Warwickshire rhyme illustrates:

When candles burne both blue and dim,
Old folks will say, "Here's fairy Grim."[4]

In other words, when a candle burned with a strange blue flame, the Grim Reaper would be on his way to collect a life, or he might come "screeching like an owl" at the windows of the sick and dying.

In Yorkshire, there are church grims who live inside the building and haunt the churchyard in dark, stormy weather.[5] They toll the church bells at midnight when someone is about to die. Later on, during the funeral service, one of them might appear to the clergyman, who could tell from its looks whether the deceased was saved or lost: If it looked happy, the soul was in heaven; if it looked miserable, the soul was in hell.

Divinatory Meanings: The appearance of the Grim Reaper in your cards indicates a profound and inevitable change. This rarely means a physical death, but is more likely to mean a drastic ending of some kind, and a complete transformation of your way of life.

Reversed Meanings: The Fairy Grim reversed in your cards denotes an enforced or belated change, which you are resisting. Remember that all things must move and change, or they stagnate and die.

Working with Fairy Grim: Not recommended.

FIVE
FAIRY DOG/BLACK SHUCK

The Card: The upright card shows a white fairy dog with red ears, while the reversed card shows a fearsome black dog.

The Fairy: Dogs have a long history as companions to human-kind, gaining the reputation of watchfulness and loyalty, becoming the trusted guardians of both people and property. However, there are also Otherworldly dogs, and these are the guardians of magical places—the boundaries between the worlds. White-bodied, red-eared fairy dogs may appear at those threshold places where the veil between the worlds is thin and entrance to the Otherworld is possible.

In Celtic legend, Fairyland is also the realm of the dead and the afterlife. Fairy dogs often act as guides to this place, guiding the spirits of good to paradise, but they also served another role. Gwyn ap Nudd, the Welsh god of the Underworld, had a pack of fairy dogs called the *cwn annwn*, or "hounds of the underworld." Many legends of Britain and Europe tell of similar Wild Hunts: packs of supernatural dogs who fly through the night sky to pursue their quarry, and which are variously called the Gabriel Hounds, Gabble Retchets, Dandy Dogs, Yeff Hounds, and Wisht Hounds. The leadership of the hunt has been ascribed to Herne the Hunter, King Arthur, Charlemagne, Gwyn Ap Nudd, and Odin. Many have seen them on wild nights, hunting a white stag or a white boar, or more likely the souls of those humans damned for evil acts.

• • •

The reverse of the card shows Black Shuck, a phantom dog who haunts the mud flats of East Anglia (eastern England). He is variously described as having a single eye set in the center of his head, or having glowing red eyes, or even as being headless, yet having glowing red or green fiery eyes suspended in front of him. He emerges from his lair at dusk and haunts riverbanks and lonely roads, sometimes vanishing in churchyards.

When a Black Shuck appears, it is generally an omen of death, and in Norfolk it is said that no one can see a Black Shuck and live. People in lonely places have sometimes felt its icy breath on their necks, and in East Anglia, when a person is dying, it is said that "the Black Dog is at his heels." The name *shuck* is derived from *scucca*, the Saxon word for an evil spirit.

There are hundreds of black dogs all over England (forty in the county of Wiltshire alone), and they often have local names. They appear in lonely places: crossroads, bridges, old roads, deserted country lanes, churchyards, burial mounds, wells, and bridges—those places that mark the boundaries between one thing and another.

Divinatory Meanings (Fairy Dog): The appearance of the Fairy Dog in your cards indicates that it is time to pay the price of past actions, for either good or bad. He indicates justice meted out, reparation, truth revealed, and rights enforced. This may involve legal matters.

Reversed Meanings (Black Shuck): The appearance of the Black Shuck indicates sudden and violent change, troubles, upheavals, conflict, the breakdown of relationships and friendships, separation, divorce, and perhaps a change of home or job. If the surrounding cards are very badly aspected, he may indicate hitting rock bottom, disaster, catastrophe, treachery, betrayal, loss, and perhaps bondage, restriction, and imprisonment.

Working with a Fairy Dog: You can visit the Otherworld in the company of a fairy dog by taking a journey in your imagination:

Relax. You find yourself standing at the entrance to a cave, which is cut deep into the hillside. As you wonder where it leads, a strange little dog appears at the mouth of the cave. It is white with red ears and seems to glow with a radiance of its own, lighting up the passageway that leads into the mountain. You know it to be a fairy hound.

It runs a little way into the cave, and then stops and turns toward you. You realize that it is asking you to follow it. For some reason, you know you can trust this little dog, and decide to oblige.

The fairy dog guides you through the twisting rock tunnels of the mountain, sometimes turning right, and sometimes left. You realize that it is a labyrinth, and you would be lost without a guide.

Eventually the dog brings you out into a subterranean cavern, and a glittering, magical landscape lies before you. The grass is made of silver, and the trees are twisted gold. The leaves on their branches are shards of emeralds, and their fruits are round, red rubies. The roof of the cavern is a vault of sapphires, starred with glinting diamonds. All the riches of the earth are here.

A fountain rises from the rocky floor, but instead of water, it sheds drops of sparkling crystal. You feel thirsty, but nowhere can you see anything to quench your thirst. You are hungry, but the ruby apples cannot be eaten.

Strewn about the dazzling orchards are treasure chests, and you wonder what could be valuable enough to be stowed in these, in such an opulent landscape. You step forward and open one. It is full of seeds. These little pockets of potential are the real treasures of the earth. You spend some time absorbing this lesson.

When you are ready to leave, the fairy dog guides you back through the maze of passageways and returns you to the human world. Return yourself to waking consciousness.

Working with Black Shuck: Not recommended.

Six

Lhiannan Shee

"Fairy Sweetheart"

The Card: The card shows a lovely fairy woman appearing before a young poet, who awaits inspiration, quill in hand.

The Fairy: The Lhiannan Shee is a fairy from the Isle of Man whose name means something like "fairy love," "fairy sweetheart," or "fairy mistress."[6] The sole purpose of her existence is to find a human man to love her. Since she is very lovely and seductive, very few men can resist her charms, and as a lover she is very passionate, but her love comes at a terrible price. Her embrace draws both life and breath from the human, while she becomes bright and strong. The Manx fairy sometimes takes blood, too, and is a true vampire.[7]

Poets, artists, and musicians often seek out a fairy sweetheart, since she is a muse who will inspire them to write great verses, paint wonderful pictures, or sing remarkable songs. When she is absent, they cannot work, pining away with longing. When she is present, they forget all else and grow pale and thin, forgetting to eat and sleep. The lovers of the Lhiannan Shee may have brilliant careers, but will die young. Sadly, many are soon forgotten.

There have been many such men, and the legend of the Lhiannan Shee has been used to explain why so many writers, artists, and musicians burn out and die young. Sometimes men have used alcohol and drugs to find the muse, but these only hasten her departure.

Divinatory Meanings: When the lovely Lhiannan Shee appears in your cards, she indicates a fantasy relationship, and the pursuit of a mirage. She may betoken the abandonment of a good life for an impossible dream or an unsuitable person, restlessness, recklessness, or a clandestine love affair.

Reversed Meanings: The Lhiannan Shee reversed denotes an escape into daydreams, a fantasy life that ignores the real world, lost opportunities, and perhaps alcohol or drug dependence.

Working with the Lhiannan Shee: Not recommended—find a muse who does not exact the awful price of the Lhiannan Shee.

SEVEN

Fachan

The Card: The card shows a strange fairy with a red cap and only one of everything, including one eye and one foot.

The Fairy: This peculiar Highland fairy from Argyll in Scotland has one eye, one hand, one leg, one ear, one arm, and one toe; if fact, he only has one of everything, all lined up down the center of his body. He often carries a spiked club with which he attacks any human who dares to approach his mountain realm. He hates all living creatures, but especially birds, which he envies for their gift of flight.

A similar creature appears in a Welsh *Mabinogion* story: Cynon, riding through the forest, came upon a mound in a clearing. On it was sitting a huge, black man who had one foot, one eye in the center of his forehead, and a massive iron club. He struck a stag with his club, and it let out a cry that called hundreds of wild animals to the clearing. They bowed down their heads in deference, as to a lord.

There was also an Irish race of one-legged, one-eyed beings called Formorians,[8] described as the oldest inhabitants of the land, a race of wizards who intermarried with the Tuatha dé Danaan.

The fachan's pose is reminiscent of the stance of Celtic shamans, who stood on one leg and closed one eye when casting spells—one eye looks into the inner realms, and standing on only one leg symbolizes not being wholly in one realm or another.[9] Druids adopted this pose when cutting the sacred mistletoe with a golden sickle. When cutting ogham (angular letters based on tree lore) spells into staves, they would stand on one leg and use only one arm and one eye to imitate the pose of the crane, the magical bird associated with ogham, since the shape of his legs in flight is said to have inspired the letters.

Divinatory Meanings: The appearance of the solitary Fachan indicates a need to stand back from a situation in order to see it clearly, and warns against precipitous action. He may indicate a temporary retreat from the world, planning, foresight, isolation, meditation, and illumination from within.

Reversed Meanings: Business relationships, partnerships, and group enterprises are going through a testing time. You may disagree with the approach others take, and stand out as a lone voice for what you believe to be right. You feel surrounded by detractors on every side. However, the Fachan advises you to listen to what others may have to say, as their viewpoints may be valid.

Working with the Fachan: You can meet the hermit fachan by taking a journey in your imagination:

Relax. You find yourself on a marsh, surrounded by a wispy mist that swirls and dances around you. It is eerily quiet. Ahead of you, there is a faint splash, and you hear movement through the reeds. Lit by a stray shaft of sunlight stands a fachan waiting for you. You walk toward it through the mud and reeds, and it waits patiently.

As you reach the creature, it moves away slowly across the marsh, every now and then stopping to wait for you to catch up.

Eventually the mists part to reveal that you have reached a fairy island, and the fachan perches between two trees, like a sentry. You know you have to speak a password to gain entry. Speak the word that comes into your mind. The fachan stands aside and you go onto the island.

You begin to notice that the trees, stumps, and rocks are marked with symbols. Take note of them; they have meaning for you.

When you have seen all you want to, thank the fachan. Let the scene fade around you, and bring yourself back to waking consciousness. As soon as possible, write down or draw the symbols you saw. You may not understand them now, but their meanings will become clear with time.

EIGHT

BOGEYMAN

The Card: A fierce-eyed bogeyman, red and hairy, emerges from behind a suit of armor in an old house.

The Fairy: Old-fashioned parents sometimes invoked the bogeyman to frighten naughty children into good behavior, saying, "If you don't behave, the bogeyman will get you." Indeed, bogeymen have been known to steal away naughty children.

A bogeyman lives in a bogeyhole (the cupboard under the stairs), or in cellars, barns, old houses, mines, and caves—in fact, anywhere dark and dank. If you look through a keyhole, you might catch sight of a bogeyman's eye looking back at you.

They may appear as shadowy, black humanoids, but can change shape to look like black dogs, tree trunks, or beings with icy fingers and glowing yellow eyes. Usually though, the only sight of a bogeyman is as a cloud of dust. They may lurk invisibly behind people, causing an uneasy feeling, or mischievously pull the bedclothes off sleepers.

Bogeyman is also a general term for a mythical, frightening, supernatural being used to frighten the vulnerable. The word is derived from *boh*, an old Anglo-Saxon word meaning "demon," and the word *boh*, or *bo*, is a component in many fairy names. It is also a prankster's custom to creep up behind people and scare them by suddenly crying, "Boh!" or, "Boo!" This originally meant, "The devil is behind you!"

Divinatory Meanings: When the grotesque bogeyman appears in your cards, he indicates unfounded fears and groundless anxiety. You have lost your sense of proportion and are worrying over nothing. Perhaps you are more than a little oversensitive at this time.

Reversed Meanings: Depending on the position of the card, you, or someone close to you, is suffering from a highly disturbed mental state, and perhaps irrationality bordering on paranoia, or depression and despair.

Working with a Bogeyman: Not recommended.

Nine

Unseelie Court

The Card: The card shows a gathering of eight sinister-looking fairies; three of them just look like skeletons rising into the air. Two hooded figures clasp staffs, and a sinister little creature with pointed ears reaches forward. An ugly goblin wears a red cloak and has two rows of wicked-looking teeth. A female fairy with a knowing look gazes back at the viewer.

The Fairies: Scottish fairies come in two varieties: the Seelie Court, who are good and beautiful, and the Unseelie Court (meaning "Unblessed Court"), who are ugly and evil. These malevolent creatures, sometimes thought to be the souls of the damned, are usually seen at twilight and are most active during the dark half of the year, from Halloween to Easter. They live in the Underworld below the mountains of Scotland.

All sorts of monstrous beings belong to the Unseelie Court, but one particular gang of fairies is called "the Host" (*sluagh*). They travel in gusts of wind, snatching up humans and carrying them along in the melée. If someone should see them and call out a blessing, the Host will be forced to drop the unfortunate man or woman. One old man muttered, "Bless the child," and was amazed when a baby dropped into his lap. Sometimes people have been carried for hundreds of miles, and a few have even ended up in North America and have had a great deal of trouble getting home to Scotland. However, once a human has been with the Host, he or she remains under their spell and must answer their summons when it comes.

The Host takes great pleasure in forcing humans to commit wicked acts, like firing dangerous elf bolts at other mortals. In Scottish tradition, the fairies cannot throw such bolts themselves, but must compel a mortal to do so. If the victim is a friend, then the thrower can usually manage to miss, and the bolt will be found lying harmlessly beside the intended victim.

However, elf bolts are very dangerous. Being hit by one may cause a variety of illnesses, and many deaths have been attributed to them. They were often aimed at the fingers, causing the joints to swell and become red and inflamed. Some elf bolts could kill outright.

Elf bolts are small flint arrowheads, often found in Britain, Ireland, and continental Europe. In reality, the Stone Age inhabitants crafted them, but countryfolk thought the fairies must have made them to use against those who offended them. Inexplicable illnesses, like a sudden stroke, were attributed to being struck by one; indeed, the word *stroke*, for paralysis, is derived from "elf-stroke."[10]

If you can find an elf bolt, it is a lucky charm and will guard against any further attacks by evil fairies. It was once believed that it would cure wounds when rubbed on them. You should never give an elf bolt away, however, as this would be an invitation for the fairies to kidnap you!

Divinatory Meanings: The appearance of the Unseelie Court indicates a way of life overturned: unexpected change, anger, frustration, broken promises, hurt, spite, malice, jealousy, and perhaps new, but unsuitable, alliances.

Reversed Meanings: The Unseelie Court reversed indicates a low threshold of boredom and the desire to seek out novelty for its own sake, satiety, dissatisfaction, excess, and pleasures that last for only a moment.

Working with the Unseelie Court: Not recommended.

THE LADY OF THE WINTER COURT

THE BLUE HAG

The Card: The card depicts an old, wrinkled crone whose face is blue with cold. She is hooded and cloaked in withered brown. The earth beneath her is covered with snow and ice, as are the mountains in the background. A crow is perched at her feet. She carries a holly staff topped with the skull of a carrion crow.

The Fairy: This fairy is known in Gaelic as the Cailleach Bheur. Cailleach means "Veiled One" and is a Gaelic term for a hag or crone, while bheur means "blue." There are a number of other cailleachs found in Scotland and Ireland, and a variety of hag fairies in England and Wales. Fairy tales are filled with references to hags: ugly, withered old women, sometimes witches and sometimes fairies, who bring sickness, death, or winter. In English literature of the Renaissance period, the words *hag* and *fairy* were often synonymous.

The Cailleach Bheur, or Blue Hag, lives on the Ben Nevis mountain. Stones that fell from her basket formed the Hebrides islands. Her face is blue with cold, her hair as white as frost, and her cloak the color of withered foliage. She carries a holly staff topped with the head of a carrion crow and if she touches any-one with it, the person will die.

At Samhain (November 1), her powers grow and she strides across the land, beating down the vegetation with her staff and hardening the earth with frost. When her season has fully set in, she brings the snow. Then as spring approaches, her power begins to wane, until at Beltane (May 1) she gives up her struggle, flinging her staff under a holly tree, and this is why no grass can grow under the holly.[11] She then shrinks to a gray stone to wait until her season comes again. It is said that if anyone can find her staff, that person will have the power of destiny over the human race.

The Cailleach Bheur is one of the clearest examples of the folk survival of a winter crone goddess who kills the summer growth and ushers in the winter. She is reborn each Samhain, the start of winter, and proceeds to blight the earth with snow and cold. In Scottish lore, St. Brigit banishes her at the end of the season and ushers in the spring. Brigit is a Christianized version of the fire goddess Brighid, whose Imbolc festival marks the first stirrings of spring.

Divinatory Meanings: When the Cailleach Bheur appears in a spread, she indicates the winding down of a situation, end-ings, necessary change, and the end of a cycle before a new one begins.

The card may also indicate a real person: an elderly woman with intense, deep emotions beneath a calm surface. She is philosophical and appears detached, but she is utterly unforgiving of an offense against her.

Reversed Meanings: The Blue Hag reversed indicates that past hurts are still deeply affecting the questioner. He or she will not be able to move on until these have been resolved.

The reversed card may indicate a real person in your life: a mature or elderly woman with a sharp tongue, who criticizes your best efforts and is never satisfied.

Working with the Crone: The Blue Hag is much feared, but this is to misunderstand her role: she is a necessary part of the cycle of being. She brings in the winter, old age, and death, it is true, but the wheel will turn, and there will be rebirth, youth, and spring. You can meet the Crone and learn some of her lessons in the following pathworking:

Relax. You stand in a frosty landscape beneath a waning crescent moon.

Before you stands an old woman. Wisdom shines from her kindly, ancient eyes. She has seen everything and knows all the secrets. If you wish, you can speak to her and ask her questions. She may show you something or give you a gift.

Be aware of your own growing wisdom, which comes with time and experience.

The earth around you is turning to winter. The leaves are falling and the branches are showing through. The earth is going into its time of sleep.

All things must age and die; it is the way of things. But as the moon and the earth are reborn, so all things change and come to rebirth.

When you are ready, return yourself to waking consciousness.

THE KNAVE OF THE WINTER COURT

JACK FROST

The Card: The card shows a sparkling white fairy in a dazzle of snow and frost.

The Fairy: Everyone knows Jack Frost, the winter fairy who scatters ice in his wake, making the trees and grass sparkle like diamonds. He also paints windowpanes with elaborate frozen patterns and nips people's noses, fingers, and toes in his chilly grip. He always dresses entirely in white, with icicles dripping from his clothes.

Jack Frost is a creature from English folklore, the personification of the spirit of winter weather. He is one of a large number of individual fairies who control the weather: wind, storm, rain, lightning, sunshine, and so on. Jack has counterparts wherever there is snowy weather in winter.

In Russia, there is Father Frost, the soul of winter, whose icy embrace brings death to helpless travelers. He leaps from tree to tree, snapping his fingers, causing them to be covered with frost. He is a smith, binding water and earth together with heavy chains.

Some think that Jack Frost may have his origins in Scandinavian myth, where the giant Jökul ("glacier"), also called Frosti ("frost"), is the father of Snær ("snow") and the grandfather of Drífa ("snow flurry"), Fön ("snowdrift"), Mjöl ("snow powder"), and Thorri, one of the winter months.[12] In Norse mythology, such giants seem to be the personifications of the primeval forces of nature such as frost, volcanoes, earthquakes, and so on, as opposed to the forces of the sky such as thunder or rain, which belong to the gods. Giants are often said to dwell underground or have close links with the earth, just like fairies.

Divinatory Meanings: When Jack Frost appears, he indicates sudden, unexpected changes, minor setbacks, temporary chaos, minor illnesses, accidents, and mishaps.

The card may represent a real person in your life: a young man with very strong opinions, but his views shift from day to day. He is clever but inconsistent, charming but easily bored. He is good company, but don't rely on him for anything important.

Reversed Meanings: Jack Frost reversed heralds the cooling of feelings and passions, distancing from a relationship, drifting away from those close to you, and coldness toward those you previously loved.

Jack Frost reversed may indicate a real person in your life: a young man who may be attractive, but is untrustworthy. He is sly, and a clever liar.

Working with Jack Frost: You can visit the world of Jack Frost in the following pathworking:

Relax. Imagine that you stand in the narrow street of an old-fashioned village. The houses are thatched, and the windowpanes small and leaded. It is a winter's night and the snow falls steadily. You are alone—all the villagers are tucked up in bed.

Suddenly you hear a gleeful laugh, and prancing down the street comes the strangest figure. It is a little man dressed in a sparkling white costume. Icicles hang from his ears and fingertips, but these do not bother him, for he is Jack Frost himself, the prince of the winter fairies.

With mischievous delight, he paints an intricate pattern on each cottage window. Each one is different and each one very beautiful. Noticing you, he invites you to admire his handiwork.

Jack Frost shows you the beauty of the winter. Each snowflake is individual, a masterpiece of design and symmetry. The earth is covered and sleeps beneath a blanket of snow until the spring. Jack shows you the animals snug within their burrows, and the seeds waiting for the thaw to germinate and throw out shoots. But this is his time, and he transforms the human world to a fairy wonderland.

When you are ready to leave, thank Jack Frost, and return to waking consciousness.

The Queen of the Winter Court

Mab

The Card: The card depicts an exquisite female fairy dressed in fallen leaves. She floats above the floor of a wintry forest, held aloft by her gossamer wings. Her face is young and beautiful and her body shimmers with fairy glamour.

The Fairy: In English folklore, Mab is the queen of all the fay, while in Welsh lore, she is the queen of the *ellyllon* fairies. She plaits the manes of horses at night, tangling them into elf locks, and she steals human children and leaves changelings in their place.

She is often described as the midwife of the fay, and *mab* is Welsh for "baby." Her title of queen might originally have another meaning in this regard, *quean* meaning "muse" or "midwife" from the Saxon *quen*.[13] However, it was not babies she midwived, but dreams. Shakespeare wrote of her as the fairy who delivered men of their innermost wishes in the form of dreams. He said that when she roams through lovers' brains, they dream of love; when she passes over courtiers' knees, they dream of courtesies; when she passes over lawyers fingers, they dream of fees; and when she passes over the lips of ladies, they dream of kisses. According to Shelley's poem *Queen Mab*, she has power over time and can reveal the past, present, and future:[14]

> *To me is given*
> *The wonders of the human mind to keep,*
> *Space, matter, time and mind.*

Shakespeare provided a lovely, whimsical description of her in *Romeo and Juliet*, saying that "she comes in shape no bigger than an agate stone on the forefinger of an alderman." Her chariot was an empty hazelnut shell, and the spokes of its wheels were made of long spiders' legs. The covering came from grasshopper's wings, the traces were made of spider silk, the collars of moonbeams, and her whip of a cricket's collarbone. The carriage was drawn by a small, gray gnat.

While Shakespeare made Mab queen of the fairies in *Romeo and Juliet*, he replaced her with Titania in *A Midsummer Night's Dream*. Herrick and Ben Jonson wrote of her as Queen of the Fairies, while Drayton made her the wife of Oberon in *Nymphidia* (1627), though in Welsh lore she is sometimes mentioned as the wife of Gwyn-ap-Nudd.

Some writers say that she is the Brythonic (British Celtic) equivalent of the Irish goddess Mebd, or Maeve, though this link is tentative. Maeve's name means "intoxication" or "mead," a drink that in myth may confer kingship, wisdom, and prophecy. Both goddesses/fairies may have been connected with shamanic initiation.

Divinatory Meanings: Queen Mab arrives in the cards to deliver dreams, wishes, and longings as yet unfulfilled, but also new ideas, insights, creativity, fertility, and inspiration to help you fulfill your dreams. Dare to dream and dare to live the dream. Don't let others deflect you from what you truly want.

Queen Mab may indicate a real woman in the questioner's life: she is a dreamy, artistic, feminine, and reflective. She is friendly, but in a lazy sort of way. You will have to make all the effort in any relationship with her.

Reversed Meanings: Queen Mab reversed indicates—in some sense—barrenness, infertility, sterility, cynicism, and creative blocks. In some circumstances, the reversed card may indicate an unwanted pregnancy.

Queen Mab reversed may indicate a real person in the questioner's life: an unfulfilled, bitter woman who is determined to make others suffer for her unhappiness.

Working with Queen Mab: Queen Mab reveals her secrets in dreams and the symbols of the subconscious mind. If you have been performing the pathworkings in this book, you have been working with the powers of Queen Mab: the access to her realm is through dreams and visions. Now it is time to meet Queen Mab herself:

Relax. You find yourself in a misty winter woodland. It has been raining, there is a warm scent in the air, and in the sky, there is a rainbow. Standing beneath an ancient oak tree is a beautiful, winged fairy: she is Mab, the queen of dreams.

Behind her is a cunningly wrought chariot, fashioned from the thoughts of poets, with draperies woven from the dreams of artists. Two winged fairy horses stand between the shafts.

Mab takes your hand, and together you step into the chariot and prepare to ride across the Rainbow Bridge to the Otherworld. The horses flap their great wings and you take to the air.

You enter the red band of the rainbow. A soft, red light bathes you. It is the color of life . . . of energy . . . of vitality. You are drifting safely and gently upward. Absorb the red color into your aura as you drift gently up into . . .

. . . a soft, orange light. Orange light bathes you. It is the color of optimism . . . of courage . . . of joy . . . of happiness. You are drifting safely and gently upward. Absorb the orange color into your aura as you drift gently up into . . .

. . . a soft, yellow light. Yellow light bathes you. It is the color of intellect . . . of clarity of mind. You are drifting safely and gently upward. Absorb the yellow color into your aura as you drift gently up into . . .

. . . a soft, green light. Green light bathes you. It is the color of growth . . . of creativity. You are drifting safely and gently upward. Absorb the green color into your aura as you drift gently up into . . .

. . . a soft, blue light. Blue light bathes you. It is the color of healing . . . of truth . . . of protection. You are drifting safely and gently upward. Absorb the blue color into your aura as you drift gently up into . . .

. . . a band of violet light. Violet light bathes you. It is the color of dignity . . . of intuition . . . of spiritual healing. You are drifting safely and gently upward. Absorb the violet color into your aura as you drift gently up into . . .

. . . clear indigo light, which frames the gate of the Otherworld. It is up to you whether you go on or go back now. If the time is right, many secrets will be shown to you in the Otherworld, but if this is not the right time, you should go back and be thankful for what you have already been shown.

Whether you want to go back now or return later, you must return through the layers of the Rainbow Bridge: indigo . . . violet . . . blue . . . green . . . yellow . . . orange . . . red. Finally, you find yourself back on earth. Allow yourself to return to waking consciousness.

THE KING OF THE WINTER COURT
GWYN AP NUDD

The Card: This card shows the dark figure of the Welsh king of the Underworld, with his owl familiar. In the background is Glastonbury Tor.

The Fairy: Gwyn ap Nudd rules the Welsh fairies the Tylwyth Teg, or "fair folk." He is a somber-looking man, as befits the King of the Dead, and is traditionally depicted with an owl. His kingdom lies beneath the earth and it may be entered through the Welsh lakes, or through Glastonbury Tor in southwest England, where Gwyn also once ruled.

When the Christian missionaries began to convert Britain, they tried to turn people away from the old gods and spirits.

St. Collen preached against Gwyn ap Nudd, objecting to his parishioners calling Gwyn both the king of fairies and the king of Annwn, the Underworld. When Gwyn heard this, he summoned the saint to meet him on Glastonbury Tor. At first the saint was reluctant, but eventually went, armed with a flask of holy water. On reaching the hill, he found troops of minstrels, comely youths, and graceful, pretty fairy maids. King Gwyn ap Nudd, seated on a golden throne, greeted him courteously and invited him to share in the feast spread before them. The saint refused to eat the fairy food, knowing that it would condemn him to Fairyland forever, and, springing up, he dowsed Gwyn ap Nudd with holy water, which caused him to disappear.

Gwyn ap Nudd is often mentioned in Welsh poetry. He is named as the son (*ap*) of Nudd, the God of the Dead. Several fairy kings have a dual role as Lord of the Underworld and the Dead. These include Arawn, Barinthus, and Finvarra. In each case, they are derived from ancient gods of the dead. *Gwyn* means "white one," as does *Finvarra*, a color often associated with ghosts and Otherworldliness.

In Celtic lore, Fairyland and the Underworld land of the dead are usually one and the same. It is accessed through fairy mounds, tors, caves, wells, or under lakes and pools. These entrances were all sites of worship for the Celts and pre-Celts. They believed that all power and fertility, as well as life and death, came from the Underworld, which contains the souls of the ancestors, the fairies, and the gods. The dead were commemorated at Lughnasa, Samhain, and Yule when the doors to the Otherworld stood open. People who are taken to Fairyland are warned to avoid eating the food there, or they will never be able to return to the land of the living.

According to some legends, Gwyn ap Nudd leads the Cwn Annwn, the Welsh Hounds of the Underworld, red-eared, white fairy dogs of the Wild Hunt. The Hunt rides out on wild and stormy nights to pursue the souls of the newly dead. The call becomes quieter the nearer they come, but in the distance their cry is full of sorrow.

Divinatory Meanings: When Gwyn ap Nudd, King of the Underworld, appears in your cards, he indicates deeply buried secrets, things hidden, concealed fears, suppressed feelings, self-imposed restrictions, or bondage to the past. Something unresolved might be surfacing from your subconscious mind to affect the present.

Gwyn ap Nudd may be a real person in your life: a mature or elderly man of some influence who is very sober and serious, intellectual and cerebral, but impersonal and detached.

Reversed Meanings: When Gwyn ap Nudd appears reversed in your cards, he indicates power misused, abuse, obsession, violation, injury, insult, and the breaking of faith. He may also imply the profanation of spiritual mysteries: the betrayal of the sacred for personal gain.

The reversed card may refer to a real person in your life: a domineering, possessive person who abuses your trust.

Working with Gwyn Ap Nudd: You can visit the realm of King Gwyn ap Nudd in the following pathworking:

Relax. Imagine that you are walking up a hillside just before dawn. It is the night of the winter solstice. Around you, the earth and the trees are bare, except for the dark-green holly bushes bearing splashes of berries—bright-red, vital life in the midst of winter desolation.

As you reach the crown of the hill, you come upon a circle of stones, each bearing quartz crystals. They glint and shine in the predawn light.

Inside the ring is a burial mound, its entrance flanked with rocks marked with spirals, the symbol of the passage of the sun around the earth and its daily and yearly death and rebirth. As you watch, the mound opens. It is dark and silent inside.

Then you hear the muffled sound of the baying of many dogs. Behind you, riding through the sky, is King Gwyn ap Nudd and the Wild Hunt. He is mounted on a coal-black horse, accompanied by the *cwn annwn*, his fairy dogs. You step aside as they enter the mound, home from the night's hunting.

It is getting light now as you follow them inside the chamber within the mound. You know it is a burial chamber, but you are not afraid. It seems quite peaceful and a place of promise—more like a womb than a tomb.

Suddenly, a shaft of bright light illuminates the chamber. It is the light of the newly risen sun hitting the tunnel of the mound and shining down into the inner chamber, filling it with radiance and energizing the resting spirits within.

You feel the light and warmth on your skin, penetrating the cells of your body, and entering the very core of your being. The illumination fills you, revitalizing every part of you, and making you feel full of life and vitality. You feel the possibilities of life, the newness of everything. With the reborn sun, you are reborn, a child of light and promise. From this point on, you can make a new beginning. All is possible for you.

Take some time to explore this feeling. Bathe in the radiance. From his throne, which is outlined in the light, Gwyn ap Nudd raises his cup in homage to you. You bow to him in return. If you wish, you may spend some time feasting with the fairies inside their mound.

After some time, you leave the chamber. Outside, morning has begun. A bright, winter light illuminates the landscape. You become aware that the day is fresh and newborn. A new time has begun. Your new energy makes you want to seize the moment to fulfill the promise of your life.

When you are ready, return yourself to waking consciousness.

1. Wirt Sikes, *British Goblins: The Realm of the Faerie* (1880; reprint, Llanerch facsimile edition, 1991).

2. Thomas Keightley, *The Fairy Mythology* (London: Whittaker, Treacher and Co., 1833).

3. Amabel Williams Ellis, *Fairy Tales from the British Isles* (Glasgow and London: Blackie, 1976).

4. Roy Palmer, *The Folklore of Warwickshire* (London: Batsford, Ltd., 1976).

5. William Henderson, *Folklore of the Northern Counties* (London: Folklore Society, 1879).

6. She has counterparts in the Irish leanan sidhe, leanhaun shee, or leannán sí, and the Scottish leannan sith.

7. W. B. Yeats, *Folk and Fairy Tales of the Irish Peasantry* (1888).

8. Peter Lamborn Wilson, *Irish Soma* (www.lycaeum.org/~lux/ features/ irshsoma.htm).

9. John Matthews, *Taliesin* (London: Aquarian Press, 1991).

10. Crofton Croker, *Fairy Legends and Traditions of the South of Ireland* (London: John Murray, 1826).

11. Donald A. Mackenzie, *Scottish Folk-Lore and Folk-Life* (London: Blackie, 1935).

12. Andy Orchard, *Dictionary of Norse Myth and Legend* (London: Cassell, 1997).

13. Larousse, ed., *Larousse Dictionary of World Folklore* (Edinburgh: Larousse, 1995).

14. Percy Bysshe Shelley, *Queen Mab*.

The Fairy Festival Cards

Using the Fairy Festival Cards

The festivals most associated with the fairies are the four fire festivals of the Celts, and the solstices and equinoxes universally celebrated by ancient Pagans. It may be that in the stories of the fairies and their activities we can trace remnants of the religion of the old gods. It is difficult to draw a line and say where the old animistic nature spirits end, and gods and goddesses begin.

The eight cards of the Fairy Festivals represent powerful energies entering or leaving the current life cycle of the questioner. They should be given extra weight in any reading.

The four cards of the solstices and equinoxes (Ostara, Midsummer, Herfest, and Yule) depict magical fairy islands, while the four pastoral cards (Imbolc, Beltane, Lughnasa, and Samhain) are illustrated with fairy mounds. All of the eight cards depict some of the fairies associated with the season.

IMBOLC

The Card: The card depicts a fairy mound at the beginning of February. The trees are frosted white and patches of snow lie upon the ground. Winged fairies peer down from the trees, while in the foreground a Hag fairy sweeps the ground with a broom. From the fairy mound, ethereal white spirits issue in spirals of light. The moon stands at a slender crescent.

The Festival: Imbolc, celebrated on February 1, was one of the four pastoral festivals of our Celtic ancestors. It celebrates the very first stirrings of spring, when the sap rises in the trees and snowdrops poke their heads through the snow.

The Celts marked it as the festival of the goddess Brighid, who was later Christianized as St. Brigit. She carries a white willow wand, and with it, she regenerates the lifeless land, bringing back the green shoots and engendering a new round of birth among animals. At Imbolc, the first lambs of the year are born—a powerful symbol of renewal, innocence, and purity. In folktales, Brighid appears in fairy form to chase away the Hag of Winter and bring back the spring. In some tales, the Hag and her rival, the maiden, fight in the forms of dragon and lamb. In Scottish lore, the adder, representing the power of the Cailleach, is defeated by the lamb of Brighid.

In ancient times, this yearly defeat of winter was marked by a women's festival. The married women of the tribe would paint themselves with woad and go naked to the festival site to honor the Crone, while the younger women would gather gifts to offer at Brighid's shrine.

In January and February, the earth is washed by the winter rains. The ancients believed this to be the ritual purification of the Earth Goddess after giving birth to the new sun at the winter solstice. The Roman feast of Februa (giving its name to February) took place at this time, when women would undergo purification after parading through the streets carrying candles. The festival was Christianized as Candlemas, marking the purification of the Virgin Mary after giving birth to Christ. During the mass, the church candles were blessed. Candles play an important part in many religions, symbolizing light. After the winter solstice, the light begins to increase, and the days have lengthened considerably by Imbolc.

At Imbolc, many fairies come out of their winter resting places to test the weather. If it is still cold and frosty, they will retreat for a little longer. The Manx fairy Caillage Ny Groagmagh ("Old Woman of Gloominess") looks out at Imbolc. If the weather is fine, she takes the form of a giant bird to gather firewood to warm her through the summer. If it is wet, she stays in, and because she has no firewood, she has to make the rest of the year sunny in order to dry the wood. In Ireland, the People of the Hills leave their mounds and move among human beings.

Divinatory Meanings: When the Imbolc festival card appears in a spread, it indicates potent energies of resurgence, purification, freshness, originality, and new beginnings.

Reversed Meanings: The reversed card indicates stagnation, stalemate, a lack of progress, boredom, decline, and depression.

OSTARA

The Card: The card shows a mysterious fairy island. Fairy islands appear and disappear in the twinkling of an eye, and may never be seen in the same place twice, though a few lucky humans have been able to visit them. It is the spring equinox, also called Ostara, when many fairies emerge from their winter hideaways. Some of them can be seen on the cards, such as the formidable woodwose and the pretty, winged fairy in the foreground. Early daffodils decorate the foreground.

The Festival: At the spring equinox—called Ostara by the Saxons—the days have noticeably lengthened. Day and night are of equal length, but the light is gaining and spring has really arrived. Birds are busy building nests and young animals are mating. Green leaves appear on the trees, and drifts of daffodils appear in the hedgerows.

As the weather starts to brighten, some good fairies emerge from their winter hideaways and others become more active. Some shed their winter skins and adopt a fresh guise for the coming summer. If fairies are denied their rightful portion of the festival feast, you will have to give them twice as much at Midsummer, or you will be troubled until the next Ostara.

Many fairies are associated with vegetation, crops, and the fertility of the land, with the power of either blessing or blighting. These fairies may be directly related to ancient vegetation spirits. In winter, the spirit of vegetation seems to die, to go down as seed into the earth until it is resurrected the next spring. Ancient religion was largely concerned with entreating the gods and nature spirits to provide the harvest. It was often thought that when fairies awoke in the spring, a sacrifice should be made to them, perhaps an offering of milk, honey, cream, melted butter, or in some cases, a cock.

In Britain and elsewhere in Europe, the vegetation spirit is portrayed as the Green Man or woodwose at spring festivals, a symbol of regeneration, vegetation, life, and hope.

At the equinox, many fairies bathe in rivers and streams. It is safer for humans to stay away from such places, or the fairies might take them away or drown them in the water.

Divinatory Meanings: When the festival card of Ostara appears in a spread, it heralds dawning creativity, emergence, an in-pouring of energy and ideas, versatility, dexterity, idealism, and individuality. An idea or situation begins to crystallize and take form.

Reversed Meanings: The reversed card denotes restlessness, wasted energy, rashness, impatience, superficiality, indecisiveness, thoughtlessness, and inconsistency.

BELTANE

The Card: The card depicts a fairy mound on May Eve, surrounded by reveling fairies holding little lanterns. Above the mound is a large full moon, and outlined against it stands the Fairy Queen of the mound holding a golden cup. In the foreground is a little, green-skinned fairy with pointed animal ears.

The Festival: May Day is the first day of May and marks the start of summer in many countries of the Northern Hemisphere; the ancient Celts called it Beltane and started the celebrations on May Eve. In England, May Day was, and still is, celebrated with morris dancing, circling the maypole, and gathering hawthorn blossoms from the greenwood.

A number of fairies become industrious around this time, particularly those associated with vegetation, the spring and summer, and forest spirits such as Puck and Robin Goodfellow. Fairies may occasionally be glimpsed going about their business at Beltane. It is a very magical time, and anyone sleeping beneath a solitary hawthorn on May Day is liable to be kidnapped by fairies, or accidentally slip into Fairyland.

The Cailleach Bheur, a Scottish winter hag whose powers wane with the onset of spring, finally gives up her struggle against the summer, flinging her staff under a holly tree, and shrinks to a gray stone to wait until her season comes again. In Leicestershire (England), the Black Annis Hunt was once held every May Day to chase the summer hare. Black Annis is a Midland winter hag fairy, and the hunt symbolized the end of her winter reign and the start of summer. In Celtic cultures, it was taboo to hunt the sacred hare at any other time.

In Arthurian legend, Guinevere, thought by many to be of fairy origin, rode out a-Maying to collect greenery and hawthorn flowers from the greenwood. She may be a later form of the Welsh goddess Blodeuwedd, who began life as a maiden composed of flowers and finished as an owl (a "white phantom"), as befits a seasonal goddess of life and death.

May Day is also connected with Robin Hood; in fact, in England it was called "Robin Hood's Day." He was an outlaw of the greenwood who dressed in Lincoln green and may perhaps have been a spirit of the forest himself. In Britain, some of the ancient nature spirits and gods passed into lore as woodland fairies, often given the name of Hob, Robin, or Robin Goodfellow, and this may be the real origin of the legends of Robin Hood. Consider his name, his green clothing, his forest home, and his deadly arrows; perhaps he was the nature god of the ordinary people who could seek him in the forest.[1] In some traditional witch covens, the Lord is addressed as Robin and the Lady as Marian.

Divinatory Meanings: When the Beltane festival card appears in a spread, it heralds mighty forces of strength, blossoming, flourishing, growth, happiness, love, marriage, new relationships, virility, energy, and fertility.

Reversed Meanings: The reversed card betokens weakness, infirmity, impotence, illness, disintegration, and dissolution.

Midsummer

The Card: The card shows a clear Midsummer Day, a time when many fairies visit the human realms. Some of them can be seen in the picture, including Aine and Robin Goodfellow. A fairy bard provides the music for their revelries. In the background, the fairy island seems closer to the shore, as this is one of the magical days when it can be accessed by humans.

The Festival: Midsummer is one of the most ancient festivals, derived from Pagan celebrations of the summer solstice, and Christianized as St. John's Day. The day marked the peak of the sun god's power, the longest day before his decline and "death" at the winter solstice. Midsummer Day is now celebrated on June 24, while the solstice usually falls on or near June 21 in the Northern Hemisphere.

Midsummer Eve is one of the most mystical times of the year, when all sorts of magic and enchantments are in the air. Nymphs walk the land, and where they walk, flowers appear. Spirits and fairies are abroad, moving among humankind, frolicking around the Midsummer bonfires, and playing all sorts of tricks ranging from innocent pranks to inflicting horrible curses and even death on those who offend them. It is at this time that they most often steal away human women to become their brides.[2]

They love to visit certain magical places, such as the Rollright Stones in Oxfordshire (England) where they pop out of a hole near the King Stone and dance around the circle. Fairy mounds open and the little people come forth to dance to their lovely, unearthly music in the moonlight. But beware: any human who joins them in their ring will be forced to dance with them forever.

The mischievous fairy called Robin Goodfellow, Jack Robinson, or Puck plays tricks on the unwary who dare to venture out into wild and lonely places on such an enchanted night. He is believed to light the Midsummer bonfires himself. In parts of Worcestershire, peasants claimed to be "Poake led" into ditches and bogs by the mysterious fairy before it disappeared with a loud laugh.

In the Shetlands, those strange and lovely creatures called selkies come ashore on Midsummer Eve. They normally have the appearance of gray seals, but shed their skins to become human on this night. Once ashore and in human form, the selkie folk will dance on the seashore, and if they are disturbed, they will grab their skins and run back to the sea.

In Somerset, little fairies called spunkies appear like will o' the wisps, carrying candles and leading travelers astray. On Midsummer Eve, they go to the churchyard to meet the newly dead. Some say that the spunkies themselves are the souls of unbaptized children, condemned to wander until doomsday.

The Irish fairy the Amadan-na-Briona is at his most active at Midsummer, playing mischievous tricks on people. Also called "the Fool of the Forth," he changes his shape every two days. When he appears as a man, he is very wide and wears a high hat, though he has been known to appear as a sheep with a beard. If you meet him you should say, "The Lord be between us and harm," because if he touches you, he will inflict an incurable madness or even death.[3] He knocks on doors late at night, throwing bowls containing blood at people, or he pops up from behind hedges.

Traditionally, the best time to see fairies is on Midsummer Eve.

Divinatory Meanings: The Midsummer card ushers in joyful energies of magic, enchantment, consummation, culmination, celebration, delight, fun, light, illumination, and clarity.

Reversed Meanings: The reversed Midsummer card indicates oversensitivity, muddled thinking, solitude, exclusion, a lack of communication, dejection, and misery.

Lughnasa

The Card: The card shows a fairy mound against a red-streaked sky at sunset. In the background is a field ready for harvesting, and in the foreground are ears of corn and chamomile flowers. A young fairy clad in green leans against a tree, wearing a chaplet of flowers about her head. Spriggans and animal-eared fairies hang in the trees with lanterns.

The Festival: Lughnasa is one of the fairy festivals. It marks the start of the grain harvest and was Christianized as Lammas, or "loaf mass," when bread made from the first harvested grain was offered up in the Eucharist ritual.

    Several fairies become animated at this time and are particularly interested in the harvest, trying to steal the grain or kicking harvesters who have fallen asleep in the sultry heat of the day. In Britain and Ireland, fairies hold processions or move house at Lughnasa, and sometimes a line of lights can be seen moving from one hill to another.

Lughnasa was named after the god Lugh, who is sometimes compared to the Roman Mercury. He was a king of the Tuatha dé Danaan and introduced the festival to commemorate his foster mother Tailtu, a daughter of the Firbolg king and an agricultural deity who expired after clearing a forest. The festival took the form of funeral games, similar to the original Olympics. Lugh once fought a battle with Balor, the Dark One, and originally the battle may have been an annual one between summer and winter, the forces of light and the forces of dark, since Lughnasa is considered to be the end of summer and the first day of autumn.

Faction-fighting was a customary feature of many Lughnasa assemblies. Groups of young men from rival villages would gather and fight. Faction-fights could be fierce and lead to injuries and occasionally death; but it was the observance of the custom that was considered to be important, rather than winning at all costs. The opposing teams would kiss or shake hands as friends afterward. There is a strongly held belief in Irish folklore that the success or failure of the harvest was dependent on the fairies, and was decided by a battle between two troops from neighboring areas. This idea that success in battle brought fruitfulness to the crops of the winning side is probably the origin of faction-fighting. It is possible that these fights were symbolic reenactments of these fairy battles.[4]

A feast day of the fairy Aine occurs at Lughnasa. She was originally a goddess of the harvest, and the first Friday, Saturday, and Sunday after Lughnasa are sacred to her. It was said that she would claim a human life on those days, perhaps a folk memory of the days when a sacrifice was made to ensure the safety of the harvest.

The Irish fairies the sidhe are probably descended from such old gods as Crom Cruaich ("the Crooked One of the Hill"), whose festival was on August 1, Lughnasa. Like the fairies, he lives in the ancient burial mounds. He was originally an agricultural/Underworld deity who controlled the ripening of the crops and the fertility and milk yield of cattle. To this end, offerings were made to him so that he would not blight the corn and spoil the milk. Into living memory, offerings were similarly made to the sidhe for the same purpose, with milk and butter being placed on the fairy mounds.

Divinatory Meanings: When the festival card of Lughnasa appears in a spread, it indicates that you will start to reap the rewards of your efforts, though more work is needed to bring a project to final completion. The card may also indicate that the closing of one door will lead to the opening of another.

Reversed Meanings: When the card of Lughnasa appears reversed, it indicates ingratitude, thanklessness, fruitless effort, and a lack of recognition.

Herfest

The Card: The card shows a group of fairies at the autumn equinox, which is also called Herfest, the harvest festival. Corn stands ready to be harvested, and in the foreground is a Poppy Fairy, with flowers in her hair. A fairy hunter, armed with bows, stalks his prey, while in the background the fairy island is hidden in mist.

The Festival: Herfest ("Harvest Festival") is celebrated at the autumn equinox, and, in Britain and Ireland, it marks the major harvest. Light and darkness stand in balance, with equal hours of night and day; but the darkness is gaining, and with it, barren winter. This is symbolized by the battles between such fairies as the Sea Mither and Teran, who represent summer and winter, respectively.

Fairies are very interested in the reaping of the grain and are determined to have their share. Farmers once made special efforts to placate mischievous or malicious fairies in order to protect the crops. The harvest was fraught with tension. The weather might ruin the grain, the work was hard, and the final capture of the Corn Spirit was hazardous. This vegetation spirit had to be treated carefully to ensure a full rick. As late as the beginning of the twentieth century, the harvesters followed customs that would have been familiar to the ancient world. The corn was cut in decreasing circles, the Corn Spirit ever retreating into the remaining ears. There was a reluctance to be the one to cut the final ear and be the captor of the spirit, so sickles were thrown at it from a safe distance.

Getting the harvest home safely was a time of great relief and a cause for celebration. A feast would be held for all the workers with an abundance of good food and drink and was probably the best meal the laborers would enjoy all year. The doors and gates of the farm were decorated with greenery, grain, flowers, and ribbons, and wreathed scythes and sickles would be placed in the arches of the house. You can be sure that on many farms, offerings of food and drink were left out for the fairies.

The final sheaf to be cut, which embodied the Corn Spirit, would be fashioned into a corn dolly and kept safe until the following year, when it would be plowed into the ground to return the vegetation spirit to the earth.

Divinatory Meanings: The festival card of Herfest indicates fruition, completion, harvest, reward, recognition, success through hard work, and bounty.

Reversed Meanings: The reversed card indicates poverty, lack, loss, failure, unprofitable speculation, financial problems, and bankruptcy.

Samhain

The Card: The card shows a fairy mound at night, with a sickle moon hanging in the sky. Light streams from the mound, since this is the night it opens and human visitors might gain access. The trees are hung with jack-o'-lanterns. Skeletons also perch there, and bats fly about the sky. In the foreground are fly agaric mushrooms and two red-clad fairies, one of them winged.

The Festival: This ancient Celtic festival, known in modern times as Halloween, is celebrated at the beginning of November. The hours of light have diminished; the days are short. The powers of growth and light are in decline, and the powers of darkness and cold begin to gain ascendancy. Similar festivals are celebrated around the world, marking the start of winter and the dominion of the powers of blight, decay, and death.

Samhain was the Celtic New Year and marked the beginning of winter. For the Celts, any boundary was important magically. These times and places were dangerous: one might enter Fairyland through them accidentally, or aspects of the Otherworld might pass through into our own. The time when one season passed to another was particularly tricky, especially the two hinges of the year, Beltane (May Day, the start of summer) and Samhain, when the Otherworld came very close. Samhain is the pivotal point of the year itself, when one year passes to the next and the doors between the worlds stand open.

At Samhain, the cattle were brought down from the summer pastures to the safer lowland winter ones. Any beast that could not be kept through the winter would be slaughtered. This is one of the reasons Samhain was called "the Festival of the Dead." Some of the animals would have been ritually sacrificed to appease the powers of winter (like Irish offerings at Samhain to the Formorians, gods of blight) and to feed the spirits of the dead that came to visit the Samhain feast.

After Samhain, ghosts, spirits, and evil fairies walk the land. Good fairies, such as the Irish Tuatha dé Danaan and the English Puck, retire from sight until spring returns. Wicked fairies, such as the Scottish Unseelie Court, become very active from now until Easter, along with cailleachs and hag fairies, who were probably once crone goddesses of winter who ruled over the season. Evil omens such as black dogs also appear. Fairy mounds open at Samhain, and you might get a glimpse inside. At Hollantide (November 11, Old Samhain), the Hillmen, or Hogmen, the most feared of the Manx fairies, move their abode, and humans should not venture out then.

After Samhain, all the crops left unharvested belong to the fairies. In Ireland, Halloween is called Phooka Night, and after this the fairy Phooka renders all the crops unfit to eat and spoils all the blackberries. Welsh gryphons blight any crops left in the field. The lunantishees ("moon fairies") will not allow blackthorn to be cut on November 11 (Old Samhain before calendar changes).

Divinatory Meanings: The card of Samhain indicates powerful forces at work leading to endings, change, the completion of a cycle, dissolution, and winding down. It may also mean ancestral contact, family or tribal ties, clairvoyance, and mediumship.

Reversed Meanings: The card of Samhain reversed indicates immobility, quiescence, constriction, and censure.

YULE

The Card: The card shows some of the many fairies associated with Yule, the winter solstice, including Father Christmas and one of his elves, along with Jack Frost, who brings the icy weather. The fairy island floats, dark and brooding, in the background.

The Festival: Yule is the midwinter festival, the winter solstice, falling on or near December 21 in the Northern Hemisphere. It is the longest night of the year and the shortest day, when the ancients believed that the powers of darkness held sway. Fires were lit as a form of sympathetic magic to encourage the "rebirth" of the sun. After the solstice, the hours of daylight increase, minute by minute, until the summer solstice, the shortest night and longest day.

Father Christmas, or Santa Claus, is a very special fairy who appears only once a year. It is possible that he evolved from the Scandinavian/Germanic god Odin, or Woden, who rode the skies at Yule wearing a red, bloody, flayed animal skin, punishing the wicked and rewarding the good. It seems likely that he passed into English folklore, and can be traced in the character who appears as master of ceremonies in the mumming plays and as the King of Christmas. In Germany and Austria he was transformed into the *Schrimmerlreiter* ("White Horse Rider"). He entered North America with the Dutch Sante Klaas, anglicized as Santa Claus.[5] Similar gift-giving fairies include Icelandic Jola Sveinar, the Danish Julenisse, and the Swedish Jultomte.

Several fairies destroy any spinning left on the wheel at Yule or Christmas. This has its origin in the fact that many sun gods and goddesses were associated with the spinning wheel of the sun, which stands still at the solstice (the word *solstice* means "sun stands still"). At the midwinter solstice, all forms of spinning and weaving were forbidden. The Lapps forbade the turning of any kind of wheel, including cartwheels and churns.

Divinatory Meanings: When the card of Yule appears, it heralds powerful currents of birth, rebirth, the recovery of vitality and health, illumination, enlightenment, revelation, and a change of consciousness.

Reversed Meanings: The reversed card betokens lethargy, a fear of change, a refusal to move forward, ignorance, and bigotry.

1. Steve Wilson, *Robin Hood: The Spirit of the Forest* (London: Neptune Press, 1993).

2. W. B. Yeats, *Folk and Fairy Tales of the Irish Peasantry* (1888).

3. Lady Augusta Gregory, *Visions and Beliefs of the West of Ireland* (Colin Smythe, 1920).

4. Máire MacNeill, *The Festival of Lughnasa* (Oxford University Press, Amen House, 1962).

5. Larousse, ed., *Larousse Dictionary of World Folklore* (Edinburgh: Larousse, 1995).

SELECT BIBLIOGRAPHY

Arrowsmith, Nancy. *A Field Guide to the Little People*. London: Macmillan, 1977.

Aubrey, John. *Miscellanies*. 1696. Reprint, London: Reeves and Turner, 1890.

Baker, Margaret. *Folklore and Customs of Rural England*. Newton Abbot: David and Charles, 1974.

Balfour, M. C. *Legends of the Cars*. London: Folk-Lore II, 1891.

Berners. *The Boke of Duke Huon of Bordeaux*. Trans. Sir John Bourchier.

Bloom, William. *Working with Angels, Fairies and Nature Spirits*. London: Piatkus, Ltd., 1998.

Bord, Janet and Colin. *The Secret Country*. London: Paladin, 1978.

Branston, Brian. *The Lost Gods of England*. London: Thames and Hudson, 1957.

Briggs, K. M. *The Anatomy of Puck*. London: Routledge and Kegan Paul, 1959.

———. *The Fairies in Tradition and Literature*. London: Routledge and Kegan Paul, 1967.

Broome, Dora. *Fairy Tales from the Isle of Man*. London: Penguin, 1951.

Burton, Captain George. *Pandaemonium*. 1684.

Campbell, J. F. *Popular Tales of the Western Highlands Orally Collected.* 1890.

Campbell, J. G. *Superstitions of the Highlands and Islands of Scotland.* Glasgow: MacLehose, 1902.

Carmichael, Alexander. *Carmina Gadelica.* Edinburgh: Oliver and Boyd, 1928.

Coghlan, Ronan. *Handbook of Fairies.* London: Capall Bann, 1998.

Courtney, Margaret. *Cornish Feasts and Folklore.* 1890.

Croker, Crofton. *Fairy Legends and Traditions of the South of Ireland.* London: John Murray, 1826.

Curran, Bob. *Creatures of Celtic Myth.* London: Cassell & Co., 2000.

de Garis, Marie. *Guernsey Folklore.*

de Roquefort, B., ed. *Lanval: Poësies de Marie de France.* Paris: 1920.

Dixon-Kennedy, Mike. *Celtic Myth and Legend.* London: Blandford, 1997.

Douglas, George. *Scottish Fairy and Other Folk Tales.* London: Scott Publishing, 1893.

Edwards, Gillian. *Hobgoblin and Sweet Puck.* London: Bles, 1974.

Eliade, Mircea. *The Forge and the Crucible.* Rider, 1962.

Ellis, Amabel Williams. *Fairy Tales from the British Isles.* Glasgow and London: Blackie, 1976.

Ellis, Peter Berresford. *Dictionary of Celtic Mythology.* London: Constable & Co., Ltd., 1992.

Farrar, Janet and Stewart. *The Witches' God.* London: Hale, 1989.

Gill, W. Walter. *A Manx Scrapbook.* London: Arrowsmith, 1932.

Gregor, Walter. *Notes on the Folk-Lore of North-East Scotland.* London: 1881.

Gregory, Lady Augusta. *Visions and Beliefs in the West of Ireland.* Colin Smythe, 1920.

Grimm, Jacob and Wilhelm. *The Complete Fairy Tales of the Brothers Grimm.* Trans. and intro. Jack Zipes. New York: Bantam, 1987.

————. *The German Legends.* Trans. and ed. Donald Ward. Philadelphia, 1981.

Guest, Charlotte, and J. Jones, trans. *Mabinogion.* University of Wales Press, 1977.

Henderson, William. *Folklore of the Northern Counties.* London: Folklore Society, 1879.

Hotham, Durant. *Life of Jacob Behmen.* 1654.

Hunt, Robert. *Popular Romances of the West of England.* 1881. Reprint, London: Chatto and Windus, 1930.

Jacobs, Joseph, ed. *Celtic Fairy Tales.* London: David Nutt, 1894.

Keightley, Thomas. *The Fairy Mythology.* London: Whittaker, Treacher and Co., 1833.

Kirk, Robert. *The Secret Commonwealth of Elves, Fauns and Fairies.* 1691. Reprint, London: Folklore Society, 1976.

Larousse, ed. *Larousse Dictionary of World Folklore.* Edinburgh: Larousse, 1995.

Mackenzie, Donald A. *Scottish Folk-Lore and Folk-Life.* London: Blackie, 1935.

MacNeill, Máire. *The Festival of Lughnasa.* Oxford University Press, Amen House, 1962.

Mallory, Thomas. *Le Morte d'Arthur.* 1485.

Maple, Eric. "The House," *Man, Myth and Magic.*

Matthews, John. *Taliesin.* London: Aquarian Press, 1991.

Naddair, Kaledon. *Keltic Folk and Faerie Tales.* London: Century, 1987.

Ó HÓgáin, Dáithí. *The Sacred Isle.* Woodbridge: Boydell Press, 1999.

Orchard, Andy. *Dictionary of Norse Myth and Legend.* London: Cassell, 1997.

Palmer, Roy. *The Folklore of Warwickshire.* London: Batsford, 1976.

Paracelsus. *Treatise on Elemental Sprites.*

Pearce, Marion K. "Flag Fen Lake Village." *Silver Wheel* (February 1997).

Pennick, Nigel. *Natural Magic.* London: Thorsons, 2001.

Rhys, John. *Celtic Folklore: Welsh and Manx*. Oxford: Clarendon Press, 1901.

Scott, Sir Walter. *Letters on Demonology and Witchcraft*. London: John Murray, 1830.

———. *Minstrelsy of the Scottish Border*. 1801. Reprint, Edinburgh: Oliver and Boyd, 1932.

Shelley, Percy Bysshe. *Queen Mab*.

Sikes, Wirt. *British Goblins: The Realm of the Faerie*. 1880. Reprint, Llanerch facsimile edition, 1991.

Sinistrari, Louis Marie. *Daemonalitas*.

Spence, John. *Shetland Folk-Lore*. Lerwick, Johnson & Greig, 1899.

Tongue, Ruth, comp. *Forgotten Folk Tales of the English Counties*. London: Routledge and Kegan Paul, 1970.

Wentz-Evans, W.Y. *The Fairy Faith in Celtic Countries*. Oxford University Press, 1911.

Wilde, Lady. *Ancient Legends, Mystic Charms and Superstitions of Ireland*. London: Ward and Downey, 1887.

Wilson, Peter Lamborn. *Irish Soma* (www.lycaeum.org/~lux/features/irshsoma.htm).

Wilson, Steve. *Robin Hood: The Spirit of the Forest*. London: Neptune Press, 1993.

Wright, E. M. *Rustic Speech and Folk-Lore*. Oxford University Press, 1913.

Wright, Thomas. *Essays on Subjects Connected with the Literature, Popular Superstitions, and History of England in the Middle Ages*. London: Smith, 1846.

Yeats, W. B. *The Celtic Twilight*. London: 1893.

———. *Folk and Fairy Tales of the Irish Peasantry*. 1888.

☾ REACH FOR THE MOON

Llewellyn publishes hundreds of books on your favorite subjects! To get these exciting books, including the ones on the following pages, check your local bookstore or order them directly from Llewellyn.

Order by Phone
- Call toll-free within the U.S. and Canada, 1-877-NEW-WRLD
- In Minnesota, call (651) 291-1970
- We accept VISA, MasterCard, and American Express

Order by Mail
- Send the full price of your order (MN residents add 7% sales tax) in U.S. funds, plus postage & handling to:
    Llewellyn Worldwide
    P.O. Box 64383, Dept. 0-7387-0274-9
    St. Paul, MN 55164–0383, U.S.A.

Postage & Handling
- **Standard** (U.S., Mexico, & Canada)
If your order is:
    $20 or under, add $5
    $20.01–$100, add $6
    Over $100, shipping is free
(Continental U.S. orders ship UPS. AK, HI, PR, & P.O. Boxes ship USPS 1st class. Mex. & Can. ship PMB.)
- **Second Day Air** (Continental U.S. only): $10 for one book plus $1 per each additional book
- **Express** (AK, HI, & PR only) [Not available for P.O. Box delivery. For street address delivery only.]: $15 for one book plus $1 per each additional book
- **International Surface Mail:** $20 or under, add $5 plus $1 per item; $20.01 and over, add $6 plus $1 per item
- **International Airmail:** Books—Add the retail price of each item; Non-book items—Add $5 per item

Please allow 4–6 weeks for delivery on all orders.
Postage and handling rates subject to change.

Discounts
We offer a 20% discount to group leaders or agents. You must order a minimum of 5 copies of the same book to get our special quantity price.

FREE CATALOG
Get a free copy of our color catalog, *New Worlds of Mind and Spirit*. Subscribe for just $10.00 in the United States and Canada ($30.00 overseas, airmail). Call 1-877-NEW-WRLD today!

Visit our website at www.llewellyn.com for more information.

The Sacred Circle Tarot

A Celtic Pagan Journey

Anna Franklin
illustrated by Paul Mason

The Sacred Circle Tarot is a new concept in tarot design, combining photographs, computer imaging, and traditional drawing techniques to create stunning images. It draws on the Pagan heritage of Britain and Ireland, its sacred sites and landscapes. Key symbols unlock the deepest levels of Pagan teaching.

The imagery of the cards is designed to work on a number of levels, serving as a tool not only for divination but to facilitate meditation, personal growth, and spiritual development. The "sacred circle" refers to the progress of the initiate from undirected energy, through dawning consciousness, to the death of the old self and the emergence of the new.

The major arcana is modified somewhat to fit the Pagan theme of the deck. For example, "The Fool" becomes "The Green Man," "The Heirophant" becomes "The Druid," and "The World" becomes "The World Tree." The accompanying book gives a full explanation of the symbolism in the cards and their divinatory meanings.

1-56718-457-X, Boxed Kit: 78 full-color cards;
288-pp. book, 6 x 9   **$29.95**